# AWS

The Complete Beginner's Guide to Mastering
Amazon Web Services

## Stephen Baron

# Table of Contents

# Section 1: Introduction to Amazon Web Services

- ❖ Introduction
- ❖ What is Amazon Web Services
- ❖ What is Cloud Computing
- ❖ Advantages of Cloud Computing
- ❖ Types of Cloud Computing
- ❖ Cloud Deployment Models
- ❖ Components of AWS Infrastructure
- ❖ The AWS Infrastructure
- ❖ Understanding Amazon Business Philosophy

## Introduction To Amazon Web Services

Amazon Web Services may seem like technical buzzword to you, but there is more to it than just the name. From booking flights and hotels on Expedia to binge-watching your favorite seasons on Netflix to buying products on Amazon. All has been made possible - Thanks to Amazon Web Services, which plays a pivotal role in assisting renowned companies spread across different parts of the world such as Europe, the USA, and Asia. By 2014, AWS had a hold of 1.4 million servers and emerged as a strong competitor in the cloud computing platform.

The AWS not only provides hardware and computing resources but also renders Software functionalities. For over 9 consecutive years, The IT firm Gartner has declared AWS as a leader in Magic Quadrant for Cloud Infrastructure, proving how flexible and robust the technology is.

The first section of the book is going to highlight what AWS is, the main aspects revolving around the service, the infrastructure, benefits of running Cloud Computing on AWS and where it can be used.

## What is Amazon Web Services?

## The Origin

In the olden days, the companies had their own data centers where they had hardware resources, computers, and professional IT teams to manage the entire system, which meant that plenty of time and effort was required into the computer systems.

As a greater number of hardware types of equipment increased, the processing power also increased, resulting in higher power consumption that could put the entire system at risk. Most companies and entrepreneurs didn't have enough money to invest in the infrastructure of their own which became a barrier for companies to flourish in their respective targets.

Early in the '90s, Amazon came up with a revolutionary solution to solve the underlying problem. The Amazon CEO, Jeff Bezos put forward the idea of establishing data centers equipped with hardware resources, storage, and sufficient power so that other companies can utilize it instead of building their own data centers, which can definitely cost a fortune.

Instead of building an infrastructure from scratch, organizations can simply use the data centers provided by AWS on rent, allowing them to progress. This means that companies don't have to build their infrastructure when they can use reliable and powerful technology offered by Amazon. The data centers are widely spread across the globe. If one center fails it's easy to shift over to the data center present in another location.

## What are the uses of AWS?

AWS provides a list of services that includes hosting websites, storing data into databases, game development, IOT, and Artificial Intelligence.

Based on your company's needs, you chose a handful of services you require. These services are collectively known as cloud computing. With cloud computing, large-scale businesses no longer have to purchase and set up IT infrastructure for months. Instead, the servers can roll over in minutes using AWS.

AWS aims to provide scalable, fast and affordable services in around 190 countries.

## What is Cloud Computing?

Cloud Computing is a technical term for providing and using IT resources needed by any business. The resources range from power, storage, applications and many more that can be accessed through the internet with the pay-as-you-go pricing.

Whether you wish to store huge amounts of data or support your IT department, Cloud computing enables access to various affordable IT resources. You don't have to spend huge amounts of money on building up the hardware infrastructure. Instead, you can choose the number of resources you need, the size of the equipment and the power you require. Moreover, you can have access to as many equipment and pay accordingly no matter where you are.

Through a cloud services platform, you can gain access to databases, servers, storage and a set of application services easily using the World Wide Web. The AWS is a highly flexible and reliable cloud computing platform that is responsible for managing the hardware resources. The resources aren't noticeable to the user as the cloud platform offers a degree of abstraction which may differ from virtual hardware to complex systems.

## Advantages of Cloud Computing

❖ **Saves Money**

First and foremost, you don't have to invest in building up your data centers when you can remotely access the data centers offered by AWS via a cloud platform. You only pay for the resources that you consume. This will cut down the cost of buying expensive hardware and managing it.

❖ **Agile**

By agile, we mean that you can easily access the IT resources in the comfort of your home. Wherever you are, the resources will be made available in seconds without any delays. The cost, as well as time, is saved.

❖ **Capacity**

Before you purchase any system/application, you estimate the storage that you need and see which one is suitable for your needs. It's very difficult to make a sensible decision based upon the estimation. Sometimes, a user may end up with a very expensive system that wasn't necessary or purchases a system with limited functionalities. However, with cloud computing, you don't have to worry about making prior decisions. The scalability increases, which means that you can either use as much or fewer capacity depending upon your needs in real-time.

❖ **Cuts down the cost of maintaining data centers**

The time needed to maintain and manage the data centers is eliminated since it's in the hands of the cloud service provider. You only have to focus on your business instead of looking after the infrastructure.

❖ **Easy Deployment**

You're a click away to deploy your application across the globe within minutes. This eliminates delay and provides a satisfying experience for the clients, that too, at a lower cost.

## Different Types of Cloud Computing

The Cloud computing platform helps the IT departments to focus on what's important and what's not. There are different models and strategies offered by Cloud Computing, all aim to satisfy the needs and wants of the user. Every Cloud Computing model varies from one another depending upon the flexibility, deployment, and control. It's important to understand the infrastructure as a Service, Platform as a Service and Software as a Service. They are discussed below:

❖ **Infrastructure as a Service**

The infrastructure includes resources like storage, computers, networks, and servers that are the basic building blocks for cloud computing. In IaaS, you've got greater control over your hardware resources. So, if you want to create an application from scratch, you'll need IaaS to begin with.

### ❖ Platform as a Service

In PaaS, you're free from the responsibility of taking care of the hardware infrastructure so that you can focus on the management and deployment of your applications on the cloud. There is no need to worry about patching, maintaining your applications, planning storage, procurement, and any other administrative tasks.

### ❖ Software as a Service

SaaS provides a customized application/software that is offered and managed by the service provider. In simpler words, any end-user application that can be used to perform any task. For example, a web-based email would allow you to send and receive emails without looking into the backend working of the application. You don't have to manage the application nor the servers since it's the duty of the service provider.

AWS is one of the cloud providers that is offering three types of cloud computing, as listed above.

# Cloud Deployment Models

## 1. Cloud

An application is deployed in the cloud-based infrastructure. The applications stored in the cloud could either be made on the same platform or could be imported from another infrastructure. The applications made in the cloud can be built on ordinary hardware resources or high-level infrastructure having some level of abstraction to hide the complexity of the hardware from the end-user.

## 2. Private Cloud

As the name says, the private cloud is a cloud-based architecture used by organizations. Any person belonging to an organization can have access to the cloud, whereas outsiders don't have access rights, thus increasing the security of the system. The private cloud-based infrastructure is perfect for organizations that are concerned about security and management.

## 3. Public Cloud

Contrary to Private Cloud, this type of cloud service is open for the public, provided that the end-user pays for the resources used. Amazon Web Services is a public-based cloud that allows any business to grow and make use of their applications, storage, etc.

## 4. Hybrid Cloud

This type of model combines Private and public clouds. However, they can work independently of each other as well. In this service, not only internal entities play the role but the external users can also provide resources, enabling the communication between both of them. The Hybrid Cloud is suitable for adaptability, security, and scalability.

AWS is an on-demand public cloud that has indeed become significant in IT departments of every organization. It's one of the largest providers of cloud computing technology. With AWS, developers can fire up their applications in no time. What's spectacular about this service provider is that it has more than 150 services ranging from auto-scaling to deployment options to features that aren't available in other cloud platforms.

AWS has server-less programming, leaving behind the server construct. When you're in the AWS cloud, you can make choices against an array of APIs using code or software embedded within the application.

## Components of AWS Global Infrastructure

AWS is catering its services to millions of users in more than 190 countries and is steadily growing its infrastructure to accommodate the user's requirements and ensure data integrity. AWS continues to provide a flexible infrastructure that fulfills the global needs of the users.

The AWS infrastructure encompasses regions and availability zones. A region is a geological location in any part of the world where AWS has multiple availability zones located close to one another. The AZ comprises one or more data centers, each having networking capabilities, storage, power, connectivity, etc. The availability zones allow you to operate your applications and databases, providing greater scalability, security, and robustness. There are over 60 availability zones in 20 geographic locations. Soon, there will be more regions and availability zones added to the list.

Every region is designed to be unique and isolated from other regions so that the stability and security aren't compromised. In addition to that, every availability zone is also separate, but the number of availability zones in a particular region is interconnected through links. You can run applications and store your data within multiple geographic locations and across availability zones within that region. Since every availability zone is independent of one another, this means that if one zone fails, you can shift to another zone without losing your data.

## Naming Conventions

To distinguish between multiple data centers/availability zones in a region, AWS has introduced a naming convention for regions and AZ.

In the table below, you can see two columns - Name and Code Name, respectively. The availability zone is denoted by a code name starting with a region name that the Availability zone belongs to, followed by a letter. For instance, the availability zones within US-west-1 could be named as:

- ❖ Us-west-1a
- ❖ Us-west-1b
- ❖ Us-west-1c and so on.

| Name | Code Name |
|------|-----------|
| US East (N. Virginia) | us-east-1 |
| US East (Ohio) | us-east-2 |
| US West (N. California) | us-west-1 |
| US West (Oregon) | us-west-2 |
| Canada (Central) | ca-central-1 |
| EU (Ireland) | eu-west-1 |
| EU (Frankfurt) | eu-central-1 |
| EU (London) | eu-west-2 |
| Asia Pacific (Tokyo) | ap-northeast-1 |
| Asia Pacific (Seoul) | ap-northeast-2 |
| Asia Pacific (Singapore) | ap-southeast-1 |
| Asia Pacific (Sydney) | ap-southeast-2 |
| Asia Pacific (Mumbai) | ap-south-1 |
| South America (São Paulo) | sa-east-1 |

## The AWS Infrastructure

What's the success story behind AWS? In other words, how has Amazon established itself into an excellent service provider and left other competitors behind? The answer is the approach that Amazon has used to develop AWS. It uses a low-margin business approach, offering highly efficient service and took fundamental steps to build its infrastructure.

## Hardware choices

Amazon purchases equipment from lesser-known companies that charge less as compared to high-end companies to build its hardware infrastructure.

The commodities offered by these companies are relatively cheaper, which you may think that the components are less reliable. It may be true to some extent, but the same can be said for top-notch equipment. They are bound to fail at some point and need replacement periodically.

One of the major challenges that Amazon has to face is evaluating high-end versus commodity components and make a choice.

A cloud service provider like AWS has a huge infrastructure size consisting of as many hardware components that needs frequent replacements in case of failures. However, Amazon also makes use of tailor-made equipment to manage the huge infrastructure, thus increasing the reliability of the data centers.

## Amazon's Software Infrastructure

AWS's Software Infrastructure is designed to be unique and commendable. Here are some of the features of its software infrastructure

### 1. Runs as a service

AWS developed a software infrastructure through which services could be provided to the users. For example, AWS had to come up with a way to use resources from a distance for the users so that the resources don't overlap with other user's resources, ensuring the security because no one would want some other user to have unauthorized access to the personal resources.

There are plenty of services provided by AWS such as sending emails, storing files, etc. So you don't have to reinvent those. Your only job is to choose the right type of services to build your applications.

### 2. Greater Flexibility

AWS makes sure that you don't have to worry about the space. It's totally up to you whether you want to increase the servers from one to thousands. There are absolutely no space limitations in the cloud. If you want to remove the excess capacity, you can easily do it within minutes. On the other hand, if your data volume increases, you can always increase the storage capacity. The mix and match feature of AWS allows customers to be innovative and use the services they need.

## 3. Offers Virtualization

AWS uses Virtualization technology in which you create a new virtual server, and after a few minutes, the virtual server boots up and is ready to use. Virtualization is nothing but cloning the functionalities of hardware or any components into a software. In this way, you could increase and decrease the resources without having to buy the actual hardware/software that would increase the expenditure. To run your applications you use the virtual server provided by AWS.

## 4. Resilient

Although the AWS hardware infrastructure doesn't always guarantee the reliability, the alternative path is to make the software resilient. Amazon has worked on making its cloud-computing technology resilient by increasing the redundancy of resources. The advantage of having multiple resources is that if in case a single resource fails to work, it wouldn't disrupt the service. For instance, if you were to store your data on a hard disk that has broken down, the data can be easily recovered and made available since AWS creates multiple copies of the data. Despite hardware failure, you can still have access to your data.

In a nutshell, Amazon has a fairly rich software architecture that allows a large number of users to gain access through the resources at stellar prices.

## Understanding the Amazon Business Philosophy

The AWS came into existence on 13th March 2006. One of the first services Amazon offered was the Simple Storage Service, aka S3 for short. The objective of S3 was to store your data on the web. The data could be media files, photos, software, etc.

When S3 was first introduced, it had limited storage capacity and was confined to only one region - the USA. Furthermore, the data storage limit was 5 GB at that time, and there were only fewer options you could perform such as read, write, and delete, which wasn't sufficient.

Following the first six years, S3 got upgraded and had expanded in different regions. The size of the storage had also increased to 5 TB and more functionalities were introduced. Any object such as data could have an expiration date, for instance: you can set up expiration date and time for the object after which you can't access the object anymore. This feature is especially useful when you want to view something for a specific period. S3 can also host websites and pages can easily be stored as objects in S3.

Later, Amazon came up with Simple Queue Service (SQS) through which messages can be passed between applications. The SQS can either accept or pass messages within the AWS cloud environment or outside the cloud. This is highly effective for building scalable distributed systems.

In 2006, Elastic Compute Cloud also referred to as EC2, came into existence that offers immediate availability of cloud computing capacity with no commitment related to the usage.

Till date, there are plenty of services offered by AWS which will be covered in this book.

# Section 2: Introduction to Amazon Simple Storage Service and Amazon Glacier Storage

❖ **Introduction**

❖ **Understanding Object Storage and Block Storage**

    a.  What is an Object Storage?

    b.  Use Cases of Object Storage

    c.  What is Block Storage?

    d.  Use Cases of Block Storage

    e.  Difference between Object Storage and Block Storage

    f.  Problems that Object Storage Can Solve

    g.  The Workload For Object Storage versus Block Storage

❖ **What is Amazon Simple Storage Service**

    h.  Basics of Amazon S3

    i.  Amazon S3 Data Consistency Model

    j.  Features of Amazon S3

    k.  Storage Classes For Archiving Objects

    l.  Get Started With Amazon S3

    m.  Introduction to Amazon S3 Access Points

    n.  Upload Files in Amazon S3

    o.  Bucket Policies

p. AWS Identity and Access Management

❖ **What is Amazon Glacier Storage**

## Introduction

Those days are long gone when a company had to build an on-site data center because now, with AWS, companies can build their digital infrastructure in the cloud easily. The AWS ensures a reliable infrastructure that you can expand or decrease according to your needs and increase your budget without making high investment on equipment.

Out of the many services of AWS, the two fundamental services that revolve around storage and security are Amazon S3 and Amazon S3 Glacier. In this section, you'll learn the core difference between object storage and block storage, learn about Amazon S3 and Amazon S3 Glacier and their uses.

# Understanding Object Storage and Block Storage

Most people often mix up between object storage and block storage. Therefore, one must understand how both of them differ from one another and its uses. An IT administrator needs to know whether object storage is suitable for storage or the latter.

# What Is An Object Storage?

Object storage, aka object-based storage, is a term that signifies how we organize and manage data as units, called objects. There are three essential components every object has, which are as follows:

## 1. Data

The data could be documents, pictures, and media files that you wish to store. The data isn't always directly mapped to documents. They can be sub-files or a combination of bits/bytes that are related to one another but not a part of any file.

## 2. Metadata

Metadata refers to information about the object such as what does it hold, where should it be used and other relevant information needed to describe the object. The person who creates the object storage is the one who defines the metadata.

## 3. Identifier

Every object is assigned a 128-bit unique identifier value, making it easier to locate your data in a distributed system. Since the physical location can be large depending upon the number of data centers scattered across the world, it will be difficult to locate your object. Therefore, the identifier is used to find the location of the object easily.

You can access your files on object storage through HTTP/HTTPS or APIs and the storage assures you that the data will not be lost.

## Use Cases of Object Storage

❖ You can store large amounts of data such as images, music, videos, etc.

❖ You can store backup files, huge databases, and log files.

❖ You can store large data sets of any organization.

## What Is Block Storage?

Block storage is the simplest and conventional form of storage that stores data in fixed-size blocks. The data is divided into blocks and each block stores some portion of the data. Every block has a physical address associated with it. What the application does is that it finds the address of the blocks and arranges them to form one complete file. As opposed to object storage, there is no metadata nor a unique identifier. The only way to locate your data is via address. It works best with transactional databases.

## Use Cases of Block Storage

❖ It's ideal for any type of databases especially transactional databases.

❖ Applications such as .Net, Java and PHP would require block storage

❖ Suitable for any mission-critical programs such as Oracle, Microsoft SharePoint, and SAP.

## Difference between Block Storage And Object Storage

There are some major differences between the technologies. In block storage, the data is divided into equal-sized blocks, each having their address but no metadata that could provide more information about the file.

On the other hand, object storage doesn't split the data into chunks, unlike block storage. Instead, the entire data is stored in the object along with the metadata and identifier. This is what makes object storage customizable and robust as compared to block storage. You can add as much metadata as you can, there is no limit. The metadata includes anything ranging from the classification of the file according to security to how important the file is. The real-world uses cases of block storage are adding photos on Facebook, storing files on Google drive, adding songs to the playlist on Spotify and many more.

Object storage doesn't allow you to edit one part of the file. Rather, you have to access the entire file and make modifications wherever needed. This can cause performance issues because whenever you want to update the file, you've to access the entire object. However, object storage has the advantage of data being stored across different parts of the world and they are easily accessible, whereas in block storage if there is a greater distance between the storage of applications, the access time increases.

Furthermore, block storage can be accessed directly by the OS, while object storage can't without degrading the system's performance.

Another reason why object storage is popular is it's designed to be highly scalable, unlike traditional file storage. You can store millions of unstructured data on the cloud.

## Problems that Object Storage Can Solve

As the growth of data increases, your storage must also increase. When you expand the size of block storage, you'll come across stability issues, constraints with the infrastructure, and complex management. Thanks to object storage for increasing scalability and solving management issues. It's one of the reliable technologies that allows you to easily locate your files according to the identifier and describes the data present in the object known as metadata.

With great scalability comes great resiliency. Now, you don't have to worry about the downtime issues because the data is always made available to you 24/7 even if one of the data centers within the region goes offline. Multiple copies of objects are stored in a large distributed system.

To check the copies against the original file, there is a unique value attached to every object, making it easier to check whether the file is corrupt or not so any corruption can be handled this way. The object storage infrastructure consists of affordable hardware in which data protection is already integrated into the architecture.

## The Workload for Object Storage versus Block Storage

Object storage works best with unstructured data that is usually read and written once or multiple times. Data sets such as images, videos, songs, and backups are collectively known as unstructured data that isn't organized nor has a standard format. It can be stored as objects.

Databases have unstructured data that doesn't require frequent read and writes. Hence, it's the best use case for object storage.

However, object storage isn't ideal for transactional databases since the data changes frequently. Moreover, it's important to note that object storage doesn't have locking and sharing functionalities.

Speaking of block-based storage, the data can be accessed as volumes by the OS. Therefore, they work well in various applications such as structured databases, virtual machine file system, and data sets that require random read/write.

# What Is Amazon Simple Storage Service (S3)

Amazon S3 is an object-based storage service offered by AWS that is flexible, fast, and secure. Thousands of businesses and companies use S3 to store large amounts of data, applications, archives, etc. Among the established companies are:

❖ **Netflix:**

Netflix is the world's top entertainment application to watch movies and TV shows. It uses S3 to store content before delivering it to a content delivery network.

❖ **Airbnb**

Airbnb is the top accommodation website that finds a place/hotel/resort for you to stay. No wonder, it makes use of S3 to store huge amount of static files, data, and pictures and perform data analytics.

Many other renowned companies have access to S3. The reason being, it's very handy, easy to use and most importantly, economical.

## Basics of S3

Let's get down to the basics of S3. The S3 objects are used as web objects, which can be accessed through the HTTP/HTTPS protocol.

Every web object has a unique URL in this format: http://bucket.amazonaws.com/key

If you've created an S3 object, it will be in the following format:

http://example.amazonaws.com/photos/ example-photo.jpg

Where the bucket name is "example" and the bucket points to the object name/key "example-photo.jpeg." Before you store data in S3, you must create a bucket. The bucket stores all the objects. When deciding the name of the bucket, there are a few rules you need to keep in mind:

- ❖ The name must be unique and shouldn't overlap with other bucket names
- ❖ Once you've created the bucket, you can't change the name.
- ❖ The bucket name should be sensible and logical that exhibits the objects residing in the bucket because, in the URL, you'll see the bucket name followed by the object.

As for the region, you can choose any available geographical region where AWS stores buckets. The object can't leave the specified region, but it can be transferred to another area.

The key refers to the object name that acts as a unique identifier to find the data. It's the combination of a bucket, key and version ID that uniquely identifies the object. A key could either be an object name or can have a directory-like format such as folder/picture/random-photo.jpeg. Note that this format doesn't represent the structure of the AWS S3.

As for the region, you can choose any available geographical region where AWS stores buckets. In the example above, us-east1 refers to the region where the bucket is located. The object can't leave the specified region, but it can be transferred to another area.

The key refers to the object name that acts as a unique identifier to find the data. A key could either be an object name or can have a directory-like format such as folder/picture/random-photo.jpeg. Note that this format doesn't represent the structure of the AWS S3.

## Amazon S3 Data Consistency Model

There are numerous data consistency models and Amazon S3 provides read after write consistency model, in which the object is read after it's created.

Let's take a simple scenario:

```
PUT  /photos/example-photo.jpg 500
GET  /photos/example-photo.jpg 500
```

The put and get commands are used to denote write and read, respectively. In this example, you write the object and read it that returns 500 response codes. Both of the commands run successfully.

Let's take another scenario:

```
PUT /photos/example-photo.jpg 500
PUT /photos/example-photo.jpg 500
GET /photos/example-photo.jpg 500
```

In this example, we are creating an object followed by another put request that overwrites the old objects' data and then a "get" request is made to read the object and return output. In this case, we have an eventual consistency which means that the "get" request can return either the first put or the second put until the change propagates. The results may not be immediate but eventually, it will be visible.

Consider this last caveat scenario:

GET /hello-world.txt 404 not found

PUT /hello-world.txt 300 (Ok)

GET /hello-world.txt 404 not found

GET /hello-world.txt 300 (Ok)

We are making a get request for the object that doesn't exist. In this case, an error will encounter. Then we make a PUT request and receive a 500 response code. The last command get is used, but we get an error "404 not found" Why is that? AWS provides eventual consistency. It will recover the first resource and then the second. If you use the get command again, you'll see that the object is successfully found.

## Features of Amazon S3

## Storage Classes

AWS offers a diversity of storage classes depending upon the usage and client's requirements. Each class provides a different purpose and is highly reliable that comes with a variable cost.

You chose a class that meets your use case scenario and requirements.

❖ **Amazon S3 Standard**

Standard class is designed for users who want to frequently access their data. It has high storage costs and a low restore cost. If you've set access time as your priority, you can opt for a standard storage class. AWS sets Standard storage class as the default class if you don't specify the storage class of your own.

❖ **Reduced Redundancy Storage Class**

The RR storage class is suitable for non-critical and reproducible data but it isn't reliable since data is prone to get lost and it's cheaper than standard class storage. If any object residing in RRS is lost, Amazon S3 returns an error.

### ❖ The Intelligent Tiering Storage Class

This isn't a storage class, rather it's responsible for moving the objects to and from storage classes depending upon how frequently the objects are used. The main aim of this storage is to optimize storage charges by automating the mechanism of moving data to suitable storage without degrading the performance. You don't have to decide where and when you should move your objects because AWS continuously monitors your data and being the intelligent tiering class, it does the job for you. If the object hasn't been accessed for long, S3 will move it to an infrequent access storage class. However, if the object in the infrequent access storage is accessed more than once, it's moved back to frequent access storage.

Amazon s3 intelligently assess the access patterns of the objects and moves them when needed. No extra charges are deducted when objects are being moved between the two different storage classes. Note that the intelligent tiering class is recommended for object sizes greater than 128 KB. If the size of the object is lesser, it won't be eligible for tiering.

### ❖ Standard Infrequent Access Storage Class

The standard IA works best for storing data that doesn't have to be frequently accessed. It has the advantage of having longer storage time as compared to standard storage.

Reliability and low delays ensure the safety of objects in the long run. The objects remain in the storage for 30 days and the minimum size should be 128KB, otherwise, Amazon S3 will charge you if it's less than the recommended size. It's particularly useful for storing backups, data and disaster recovery files since they rarely require access, but should be accessed quickly at the time of usage. You can access the data in milliseconds (same as AWS standard storage class)

### ❖ Amazon S3 One Zone Infrequent Access

Another service was introduced in April 2018 known as one zone infrequent access. It's relatively cheaper than standard IA because in one zone IA, Amazon S3 stores the objects in only one availability zone which makes it less resilient as there can be a loss of data due to unreliability of the availability zone. The storage cost is lower but it isn't as efficient as standard IA.

# Storage Class for Archiving Objects

## Amazon Glacier Storage Class

Amazon Glacier is designed for archiving data and has sufficient storage. You can either store high volume or low volumes of data, that too at a reasonable cost. Though, it takes hours to retrieve data that can put you at a disadvantage if you want to access the objects almost instantly.

Unlike S3 standard, Amazon glacier has extremely low storage costs and the objects have a duration of 90 days. If you want to access the data, there are various retrieval options such as expedite retrieval, standard, and bulk. You're charged according to the type of retrieval option you chose. If you want to quickly access your data, expedited retrieval allows you to do so in 1-5 minutes. When you've bulk of data, you can choose bulk retrieval that lets you access your data in 6-12 hours.

This type of storage has many uses such as storing archives of organizations, media resources, and backups.

## Amazon Glacier Deep Archive Storage Class

In contrast to Amazon Glacier, the deep archive storage class is suitable for storing data that is infrequently accessed. The lifetime of data is approximately 180 days, which is greater than the time duration offered by other storage classes. By default, the retrieval time is 12 hours that may be a tradeoff but considering the cost of deep archive, it's comparatively less expensive than Glacier. There is an option to choose bulk retrieval if you want to restore your data within 48 hours.

## Reduced Redundancy Storage

As the name says it, this amazon S3 storage service allows users to store reproducible and uncritical forms of data. It's designed to sustain data loss by providing the option to store objects across multiple platforms, and giving 400x times the stability of a disk drive but makes sure that the redundancy is lesser than in standard Amazon S3 storage. It's backed by Amazon S3 service level agreement. This is perfect for applications that require periodic replication of data such as any business application.

## Get Started With Amazon S3

By now, you know that Amazon S3 is a powerful storage service that lets you store and retrieve data via the cloud whenever and wherever you are. We will use the AWS management console to get started. Let's get you a quick walk-through on how to set up Amazon S3.

❖ **Sign up**

You need to have an AWS account to use Amazon S3. If you already have an account, head over to https://aws.amazon.com/s3/ and sign up for Amazon S3. You'll receive an email to notify you that your account is up and running.

❖ **Create a Bucket**

You store objects in the bucket so first, you've to create a bucket. Note that you won't be charged for creating a bucket; you'll be only charged for storing and moving objects to and from the bucket.

❖ **Open the Amazon S3 Console and click on "Create bucket"**

You'll find the bucket name field. Choose the name for the bucket. Make sure the name is unique from other existing bucket names in Amazon s3.

Chose the region of your choice where you want the bucket to be and then go to create. Congratulations you've successfully created a bucket!

## How to Add an Object to a Bucket

Once you've created a bucket, you're all set to add an object. The object could be anything ranging from documents to media files.

1. Go to the **bucket name list** and click on the bucket that you wish to add your object to.
2. Go to **upload** and a dialog box will pop-up. Click on **add files** and choose the files you want to upload.

## How to view an object

You can also see the information about your added objects. Here's how:

1. Go to the bucket in the **bucket name list**. You'll see the objects in the bucket. Tick the checkbox of the object that you want to view the information.

## How to Move an Object

If you want to move an object to a specific folder, follow the steps below:

2. Choose the bucket in the bucket list and select **create a folder**.
3. Type the folder name and choose none as the encryption setting. Save folder.
4. You'll be prompted to the name list of the objects. Choose the object that you wish to copy.
5. Go to **actions** and click on **copy**.
6. Go back to the name list and select the folder, click on **actions** and go to **paste**.

And voila, you've moved the object in just a few steps!

## How to Delete Bucket and Object

You can delete objects in two ways - either you can delete the objects separately, or you could delete the entire bucket. It's recommended to empty the contents of the bucket and keep the bucket. Once you delete the bucket, you can't reuse the name of the bucket as it may be already in use by some other user.

1. Go to the bucket name list and proceed to the bucket to choose the object you want to remove.
2. Tick the checkbox of the bucket, go to **actions** and proceed to **delete.**

## How to empty the bucket

Without deleting the bucket, you can remove the objects residing in the bucket.

1. In the bucket list, you will find the bucket icon before the bucket name. Click on the icon and choose an empty bucket.
2. A dialogue box will pop up for confirmation. Type the name of the bucket you want to empty and proceed to confirm.

## How to view the properties of a Bucket

1. Go to the bucket name list, click on the bucket and go to **properties.**
2. You'll find different attributes in the properties page such as:

   a. **Versions:** You can have more than one variant of an object in a single bucket. By default, versioning is disabled.

   b. **Tags:** A tag is a key-value pair that is used to store metadata about an object. For every resource, there is a unique tag. The main purpose of the tags is to organize your objects in a way that it's easier to track. AWS provides cost allocation tags that organize resources based on costs.

c.  **Transfer:** There is a transfer acceleration option in the Amazon S3 console. This feature enables fast transfer of files to and from at a very high speed.

d.  **Events:** A notification is sent to the user in case of any event occurrence related to the bucket. You can enable or disable it.

## How to Enable/Disable Versioning for a Bucket

1. Choose the bucket and go to the **properties** panel
2. Click on **versioning.** You'll see two options: enable versioning and suspend versioning. Choose any one option and save.

## How to configure event notification and set up the destination

Before you enable event notification, you've to set up the destination that you wish to send the notification to. Also, you've to mention the nature of the event. There are various types of events that are as follows:

❖ Object create event: Whenever an object is created in the bucket, you'll be notified if you enable object created event. All you've to do is select **objectcreated(all)** to set up the event.

❖ Object delete event: whenever an object is deleted, an event triggers to notify you that the object no longer exists. Select **objectdelete(all)** to turn this notification on.

❖ Object restore event: When there is a restore event that is generated, you'll receive a notification that tells you that the objects have successfully restored.

There are three types of destinations:

❖ **Amazon simple notification service:** It's a web-based service that handles the delivery of messages to the clients.

❖ **Amazon Simple Queue Service:** Amazon SQS lets you store large-scale data in a queue as they travel across systems.

❖ **Lambda function:** It is another computing service that allows you to upload your code so that the service runs your code on the AWS infrastructure.

You need to set up any one of the destinations before you enable event notifications for the bucket.

1. Go to the bucket, and choose **properties**
2. Go to **advanced settings** and click on **events**. In the events page, you'll see various fields: **Name, events, filter, and type**.
3. Go to **add notification**, specify the name and event.
4. Type the object name's prefix or a suffix to filter out event notifications. For example, objects having the prefix documents/ can be used as a filter. When the files are added into the document folder, a notification will be sent.

5. Lastly, pick out the **destination** of your choice.

6. For any destination, you'll have to specify the name.

# Introduction to Amazon S3 Access Points

Amazon has recently introduced a game-changing element that has made data more secure by allowing users to allocate distinct permissions to every object present in the bucket. This gives users great control over the S3 objects and makes management much easier. Access points can be created and attached to buckets so you could perform operations like uploading, updating and retrieving objects. A bucket can have around 1,000 access points, each having its own identity and access management policy.

### How to Create Amazon S3 Access Point

❖ Open the Amazon S3 console, go to the S3 buckets section and choose the bucket.

❖ On the bucket page, go to the access points table and click on create an access point

❖ Specify the name for the access point in the name field

❖ Select the network access type.

You've successfully created your access point.

# How to manage and use Access Points

1. Find the list of access points of buckets

2. Open the Amazon S3 console, go to the buckets section and choose the bucket

3. Click on the access points tab on the bucket tab

4. On the access points tab, you will find options to view the configuration of an access point, modify an access point or delete it.

## View Configuration of an access point

❖ To view the configuration details, search for the desired access point in the access point list whose details you want to see.

## Edit an Access point

1. To edit an access point, go to the access points tab and click on the options button present next to the name of the access point.

2. Go to **edit access point policy** and in the text field, enter the field.

3. Save the changes.

## Use an access point

1. Go to the access points tab and click on the options button next to the access point's name you would like to use.

2. Click on use this access point

3. To exit the access point tab, go to exit access point.

## Delete an access point

1. Go to the access point tab and click on the **options** button.

2. You'll find the delete option. Choose **delete.**

## Upload Files in Amazon S3 Bucket

After knowing the basics of how to use the AWS management console, it's time to add files to the bucket. Previously, we've discussed that whenever you upload a file to Amazon S3, it's stored as an object. An object consists of your files along with metadata that provides information about the object.

From media files to large-scale databases, you can store anything into the bucket. The maximum size limit of a file is 160 GB.

There are two ways through which you can upload files: Drag and drop and point and click. If you want to upload the entire folder, you use a drag and drop facility. However, it's supported for limited browsers (Firefox and Chrome)

When you want to upload a folder, Amazon s3 adds all the files and sub-folders into the bucket. It attaches an object key name that includes file and folder name. For instance, if you upload a folder called /documents that has two files, example1.txt and example2.txt, S3 adds the files and allocates corresponding key names to each file as documents/example1.txt and documents/example2.txt.

If you want to upload individual files and have a folder created in the Amazon S3 console, the object key name will have a folder name as its prefix followed by file name. For example, if the folder name is pictures and you upload a file named picture1.jpg, the key name will be /pictures/picture1.jpg. On the other hand, if you don't have a folder in the console, you can upload the file, and the file name becomes the object key name.

## How to upload files/folders using Drag and Drop

1. Log in to the **AWS management console** and open the console.
2. In the bucket name list, select the bucket where you want to upload your files.
3. A window will open and you've to select the files that you want to upload.
4. Drag and drop the files to the upload window. Proceed to **next**.
5. You'll find various fields such as manage users, add an account that can give access to other users and manage public permissions. Fill in the fields and proceed to next.
6. You'll see the set properties page in which you could choose the storage class and type of encryption.
   a. You can also add metadata and tags. There are two types of metadata offered by Amazon S3: **user-defined metadata** and **system-defined metadata**. The header of user-defined metadata has the prefix x-amz-meta by default. To add user-defined metadata to the objects, type the default prefix name, followed by metadata name in the header field and choose save.

b. To add **system-defined metadata** to the objects, you've to select the header such as content-type and content disposition. Type the value for the header and chose save.

c. Other properties include **tags**. You can add tags to customize the storage. Add tags to the objects that you'll upload. Simply, specify the tag name in the key field and value and save.

7. Go to next.

8. Check if your settings are correct or not before you upload the objects. To make changes, simply go to **previous**.

9. To check the status of the upload, go to **in progress**.

## How to download an object from the bucket

1. Open the Amazon S3 console and go to the bucket name whose object you want to download.

2. In the name list, tick the checkbox of the object. The information about the object will pop-up. Go to download on the bottom-right corner.

a) Or you could click on the object name, go to the **overview** tab and **download**.

## How to delete objects in an S3 bucket

1. If you no longer need an object, you can delete it. Just follow these easy steps:

2. Go to the bucket and tick the checkbox of those objects that you want to delete.

3. Go to actions and click on delete.

## How to Restore an Archived S3 Object

You can restore an S3 object that is archived to glacier and deep archive storage classes.

1. Go to the bucket and select the objects you want to restore
2. Click on the **actions** button and go to **restore.**
3. A dialogue box will pop up. Type the no of days for which you want your data to be made available for access.
4. You can either choose **bulk retrieval** or **expedited retrieval** option to restore the objects.

## Bucket Policies

You can set up a policy to an S3 bucket that handles the access rights to objects on different conditions. The policies are written in the access policy language and allow management of permissions. The permissions set to a bucket applies to all of the objects residing in the bucket.

Organizations and users can make use of bucket policies. Once the organization creates an AWS account, they have the power to control the resources, grant the permissions (read or write access) to the employees. For example, you could write a policy that gives the users read access to a specific S3 bucket at a particular time. An account has the power to allow certain users to have read and write access while allowing others to create and delete buckets as well. You can add a policy of your own choice.

The Bucket policy is different from access control lists in the sense that you can either allow or deny permissions to all of the objects in the bucket or a limited number of objects.

The bucket owner has the authority to assign a policy to a bucket. The policies may not run immediately as soon as you set them up because it takes time to propagate across the S3 service.

You can implement the policy by using the AWS console. Follow the few steps below:

1. Log in to the AWS Console
2. Go to the **bucket** where you want to implement the policy
3. Click on **properties** and then go to **lifecycle**.
4. Go to **add rule**

a. Here you set up a policy either for the whole bucket or for prefixed objects. When you're using prefixes, you can implement policies for the objects within the same bucket.

5. After you've chosen the rule, you need to configure. There are three options to choose from:

    a. Move an object to the standard IA
    b. Archive to the Amazon Glacier Storage

    c.   Permanently delete the objects

6. For this example, we will select "permanently delete" Let's just say you want to delete the object after 3 weeks. You'll type the number of days.

7. Once done, click on **review** and then proceed to **create and activate.**

Once the policy is configured, it will be applied to all of the objects within the bucket. If you've objects older than 21 days, they will get automatically deleted, whereas the new objects will be deleted in 3 weeks.

The advantages of lifecycle policy are that you can easily remove unnecessary sensitive data so as to make room for new objects and also reduces the cost. It helps to manage your storage so you don't have to worry about data taking unnecessary space in the cloud.

## AWS Identity and Access Management

IAM is a web service offered by AWS that enables access management to AWS resources. With IAM, you can create users and groups and allocate permissions to allow or reject their access to the resources.

When you create your AWS account, you're the root user that has the entire access to resources and services. Since you have the authority over the account, only you could grant permission to users to use the resources in your account.

## Features of IAM

❖ First and foremost, you can give permissions to users to use the resources and services in the account without having to share your credentials

❖ You can give different permissions to different people for accessing various resources. For instance, you can allow specific users to access Amazon S3 and other services. For others, you can allow write-only access to the buckets. It's up to you.

❖ AWS IAM service is an added feature of the account so you don't have to pay any additional cost. However, you've to pay for other AWS services.

❖ AWS IAM also gives access to applications that run on Amazon EC2 such as dynamo DB table and bucket

❖ Amazon doesn't compromise on security when it comes to services. IAM has a two-factor authentication option that provides extra security. You and the users not only have to enter a password but have to provide a code to gain access.

## How to USE IAM

As a good approach, don't use the root user AWS account for any task. Instead, create a new IAM user for every person and give them administrator rights by adding them into an Administrators group.

The users in the group can set up users, groups, etc for the account. All the future tasks can be performed through the users and groups. However, for service management, you've to log in as a root user.

## How to create an IAM user and administrator group

a.  Use your account to sign in to the IAM console.

b.  Allow **access to billing data** for the admin user that you will create

c.  Go to account name on the navigation bar and choose **my account**

d.  Go to **edit** and tick the checkbox to active IAM access and then click on **update**

e.  Go to **services** and return to the IAM dashboard by clicking on **IAM.**

f.  Now go to **users** and choose **add user.**

g.  Type administrator as your username

h.  Tick the checkbox next to AWS management console access and click on **custom password** to type in your new password.

i.  Go to **next** and on the set permission tab, click on **add user to group**

j.  Go to **create group** and type the group name as Administrators

k.  Open **filter policies** and proceed to AWS managed - job function

l.  Tick the checkbox for administrator access in the policy list and then **create a group**

m.  Go to **next** and you'll be prompted to **tags** page. It's optional to add metadata

n. Lastly, go to **next** and you'll see the list of group memberships. Click on **create user**.

The same method can be used to create more than one users or groups

## What is Amazon Glacier?

In today's world, storage has become a core component of any infrastructure. Everything depends upon data and so it's important to store it for future use. However, not all data needs to be available 24/7.Some data are occasionally accessed while others are frequently accessed. Inactive data that has a long-term retention period needs to be stored in cold storage called Amazon Glacier.

Amazon Glacier is a highly scalable, secure and durable form of storage that isn't heavy on the pockets when compared to other solutions offered by companies. It not only allows you to store data but lets you retrieve the data whenever you want to. The retrieval time depends on the retrieval option you choose.

## Difference between Amazon Glacier and S3

Undoubtedly, Amazon provides an array of services that can easily get one confused. Previously, you've learned about Amazon S3 which is one type of storage but how is it different from Amazon Glacier?

Both types of storage classes are durable and can be reproduced across availability zones. A huge amount of data can be stored in both.

However, there is a fine line between both of the services offered by Amazon. Their access times are different - Amazon S3 is used to access infrequently used objects whereas if you're using glacier, you store objects that don't need access for a longer period of time.

## Pricing and file retrieval options

Storing data in Amazon glacier is considerably cheaper than Amazon S3. It costs around $0.004 per GB in glacier and $0.023 in S3. Like S3, there are three retrieval options in Glacier as well. Out of which bulk retrieval is the most reasonable option. It costs $0.0025 to retrieve 1 GB of data, but the tradeoff of being the least cost option is that you'll have to wait between 6-12 hours to retrieve your data. This could be crucial especially when you need to restore the data quickly. Another option that is the standard retrieval takes around 3-5 hours. Lesser the time, the greater the price. The price increases up to $0.0.1 to retrieve 1 GB. For even faster data retrieval, you can choose the expedited option that makes your data available in 5 minutes, but that too comes at a higher cost.

## Use cases of Amazon Glacier

Amazon Glacier is widely used in businesses where storage and archiving are required. Here are some use cases:

❖ **Storing and retrieving media files**

Large-scale movies, games and other digital media files are of gigabytes or terabytes in size. Therefore, they need to be stored for long-term purposes. With amazon glacier, you can retrieve the media files whenever you want to.

### ❖ Disaster Recovery Planning

Planning for disaster recovery is a major part of any successful business. Your data needs to be prevented from corruption or any failure.

All thanks to AWS glacier, your business's data is in completely safe hands. The service lets you store a backup and restore it depending upon the retrieval option you've chosen.

### ❖ Data libraries

Libraries encompass huge amounts of data needed for future use. Thus, making it difficult to maintain the data. This is where amazon glacier comes into play - it checks the data integrity of the files regularly. There are various agencies that store lots and lots of data for future purposes. Cost isn't an issue, but durability is what matters the most. With a huge volume of data, maintenance becomes a difficult task. Amazon glacier solves the problem by checking and maintaining the files.

# Section 3: Introduction to Amazon EC2 and Amazon EBS

- ❖ Introduction
- ❖ What is Amazon EC2
- ❖ Types of Amazon E2 instances
    a.  General Purpose instances
    b.  Compute optimized instances
    c.  Accelerated computing instances
    d.  Storage optimized instances
- ❖ Instance features
- ❖ How to create an instance
- ❖ Introduction to Amazon EBS
- ❖ Features of Amazon EBS
- ❖ Types of EBS Volumes
    a.  General-purpose SSD Volume
    b.  Provisioned IOPS SSD Volume
    c.  Throughput Optimized HDD Volume (st1)
    d.  Cold HDD (sc1) Volume
    - ❖ How to create an EBS volume
    - ❖ Restore an EBS volume for a snapshot
    - ❖ Performance of EBS
    - ❖ How to create an EBS volume from a snapshot

- ❖ Performance of an EBS
- ❖ How To encrypt EBS
- ❖ How to create an EBS volume from a snapshot
- ❖ How to attach an EBS volume to an instance
- ❖ How to Delete an EBS Volume
- ❖ Benefits of EBS volume

## Introduction

One of the hardest decisions you need to make when it comes to running your applications is how many data servers are needed to meet the requirements of the users. Two scenarios could be that either you buy hardware resources more than you need or you under-estimate the requirement. In any case, you need to make a wise choice that will ultimately affect the organization. This is where AWS EC2 comes to the rescue.

## What is Amazon EC2?

Amazon Elastic compute cloud (EC2) is a web service offered by Amazon that enables users to compute capacity according to their requirements. You can either scale up or down the number of resources you wish to use whenever your requirements change. Servers are also known as instances that run applications. To put it simply, an instance is like a small part of a computer that has its network, operating system, and memory, which are virtual. You can have multiple instances in a single machine.

The Amazon EC2 lets you have complete control of the resources and run it on the computing environment. Within minutes, you can restore and boot new instances, allowing you to scale up or down the capacity depending upon your needs. You only pay for the capacity you require.

## Types of Amazon EC2 instances

The kind of computing you need depends on the nature of your applications. Instances are classified into 5 types which are as follows:

### 1. General Purpose instances

If you're new to the AWS, general instances are commonly used by the new users. They have great functionality that too at a reasonable cost. It's used for running web servers, development platforms for gaming and mobile applications and also using enterprise apps.

### e. A1

Every type of instance has a collection of instances that are responsible for handling various applications. An A1 instance is a general-purpose instance suitable for running those applications that are supported by ARM architecture such as java and python.

### f. M5

M5 instances run on Intel Xeon processors. They are much more powerful than A1 in terms of memory, computing power and performance. They are used for developing applications and testing environments. Moreover, they support Intel AVX-512, which is a series of instructions that perform encryption algorithms to provide security while keeping the performance optimal.

## Compute-optimized instance
### a. C5

C5 instances belong to the next generation of the compute-optimized family that is ideal for running computing-intensive workloads such as batch processing, machine learning, gaming, and high-level computing. The C5 instances run on Intel Xeon processors and are said to be faster than prior generations.

## Memory-optimized instances
### a. R5 and R5a

R5 and R5a are memory intensive instances that are used by applications requiring adequate memory such as large scale databases, data analytics, and other applications. There are over 48 unique instance choices you could make that have various processor options, network options, and storage options. R5 supports applications that have high memory requirements to maximize performance and reduce latency. They are designed on the AWS nitro system that delivers memory resources and computing power to the instances.

### b. X1 and X1e

X1 and X1e instances are designed for large-scale memory-intensive applications such as Presto, SAP HANA and other enterprise applications. They are powered by Intel Xeon E7-8880 processors and charge a low cost per GB of ram.

## Accelerated Computing Instances

Accelerated computing instances make use of hardware accelerators and graphical processing units to perform floating-point calculations and graphics processing. There are various instances available under in this type:

### a. P3

P3 is a new generation GPU instance that is used in machine learning, high-level computing, fluid dynamics, and analysis and recognition applications.

### b. G3

G3 instance is ideal for running high-performance graphical applications used for 3D rendering, visualizations, encoding, and streaming. It's powered by NVIDIA GRID.

### c. F1

F1 instances use field-programmable gate arrays (FPGAs) to customize hardware acceleration for your workloads. By using FPGAs, you can scale the acceleration of applications up and down. They are used in solving business and engineering problems that require high computing power, high bandwidth, and powerful networking capabilities. F1 is also useful for running real-time image processing applications and running big data analytics.

## Storage Optimized Instances

Storage optimized instances are built for applications that need high sequential read/write access to large-scale data sets present on storage.

### a. H1 and D2

H1 and D2 instances are powered by high-frequency Intel Xeon processors that offer high disk throughput at the lowest price. They are used for distributed systems, data warehouse applications, and data processing.

### b. I3

I3 instances offer non-volatile memory express designed for high sequential access, high throughput and also provide AWS nitro system for accessing resources. It's used for transactional databases of organizations, data warehousing and analytics.

## Instance features

Amazon EC2 has several features that enable the deployment, management, and scaling of your applications.

### Burstable Performance Instances

Amazon EC2 offers two types of instances: fixed performance instances and burstable performance instances, respectively. To distinguish between the two, performance instance has a consistent CPU performance while burstable performance instance has a specific baseline. When the workload increases, the burstable instance increases the CPU performance, hence it burst.

CPU credits take care of the CPU burst of a particular instance. When you're creating an instance, you'll get a CPU credit. The number of CPU credits changes per hour, depending upon the type of instance. For example, you're using a particular instance at 30% CPU performance for 10 minutes, you'll spend 3 (0.3x10) CPU credits. When you're out of CPU credits, the instances work on baseline performance that is about 30% CPU performance.

There are applications such as databases, servers and developer environment that doesn't need high CPU performance, however, they do take advantage of fast CPUs whenever they need it. If you need high CPU performance for your applications, it's preferable to choose fixed performance instances.

**Storage options**

Amazon EC2 gives you the option to choose the type of multiple storage you need for your instances. Amazon EC2 introduced Elastic block storage (EBS) which is block-level storage that stores persistent data used in conjunction with Amazon EC2. The advantage of using EBS is that your data on the system isn't lost if you shut down the server/instance. On the other hand, there is local storage that doesn't keep the data persistently on the system. There are different EBS volume types offered by AWS that will be discussed later in this section.

## How to create an instance

1. Log in to the AWS management console

2. Select the **region**. Once you've selected the region, click on **EC2** under the compute section tab. You'll proceed to the dashboard.

3. Click on **launch instance** and select an AMI of your choice. If you want a Linux instance, you can select the option.

4.  Choose the **type** of instance you need and fill in the relevant details.

5.  Go to **add storage** and click on **tag** instance.

6.  Decide the name of the instance and type the name in the value box. Whenever you open an instance, you'll see the name appearing in the console. Think of a unique name that is easy to remember.

7.  Go to **next**: configure security group and then click on **review** and **launch**.

8.  You can review the details of the instance you created.

9.  Now you've to create a **key pair**. Simply type the key pair name and proceed to **launch instances**.

10. Once you go to **launch instances**, you'll see the details of your instances.

11. Also, don't forget to download the key pair and keep it for future use.

12. Convert the private key using **PuTTY gen**.

a.  The private key generated by Amazon EC2 is in the extension **.pem** and PuTTY doesn't support it. With PuTTY gen, you can convert the private key's format into **.ppk**. It's a must that you convert your private key into this format before you connect it to your instance.

b.  Open PuTTY and go to **load** and select the .pem file of the key pair that you wrote.

c.  You'll be asked for confirmation. Click on **okay** to confirm.

d.  Select on **save the private key** to save the key in its new format that PuTTY will use.

e.  A warning will pop up about saving the key without a passphrase. Click on **yes**

f.  Type the same name of the key that you used for key-pair.

g.  Using SSH and PuTTY connect to EC2 instance.

13. Open PuTTY.exe and type the public IP of the instance in the **hostname.**

a.  In the category list, you will find **SSH**. Expand it and click **Auth**.

b.  Browse the **PPK file** that you downloaded and click open.

c.  Now type in Ubuntu when you're prompted for login ID.

You've successfully created and launched an instance!

## Introduction to Amazon Elastic Block Store (Amazon EBS)

Amazon EBS is a type of block storage volume designed for Amazon EC2 that is similar to a hard disk. The EBS volumes are like unformatted and raw block devices where you could store any type of data. These volumes can be mounted as devices on your instances. You've got the option to mount as many volumes as you want on one particular instance, however, each volume can be attached to one instance at a time. It's possible to change the configuration of the volume attached to a particular instance.

EBS volumes are highly reliable storage volumes that can be assigned to any currently active instance within the same availability zone. There is a limitation on the number of EBS volumes you can use and the amount of storage available to you.

If you want to access data quickly and want to ensure data persistence, you should go for Amazon EBS as its ideal for use for databases, applications, analytics, and file systems.

There are four different types of volume you can choose, keeping in mind where you want to use it. With low latency, you can achieve high performance of heavy workloads such as data warehouse and big data. Amazon EBS is meant for database-related applications that frequently perform read and write operations.

## Features of Amazon EBS

❖ An instance created in a specific availability zone is attached to an EBS volume in the same zone. You've to first create a volume in the availability zone. To make a volume available outside of the zone, create a snapshot which you could use to create new EBS volumes anywhere across the region, paving the way for expansion, data migration, and disaster recovery.

❖ You can encrypt EBS volumes to secure your data and applications. When an encrypted volume is attached to an instance, the data that resides in the volume, hard disk and snapshots are all protected.

❖ Snapshots are like copies of volumes. You can use snapshots to create new EBS volumes having distinctive volume types and assign them to your instances. To create backups of your volumes, you can use snapshots.

❖ You can monitor the performance of the volumes by performance metrics available on the AWS management console.

## Types of EBS Volumes

### 1. General Purpose SSD Volume (GP2)

General-purpose SSD volume is the default volume EC2 chooses that is cost-effective and at the same time offers high performance. SSD stands for a solid-state drive which is faster than Hard Disk. The performance is measured in terms of IOPS (input/output operations per second) that refers to how many I/O operations can be performed per second. The ratio of general-purpose SS is 3 IOPS with a burst value of 3000 IOPS for longer periods. It has 160 MB/s of throughput and can support 10,000 IOPS. The volume size varies from 1 GiB to 16 TiB.

## I/O credits and Burst performance

GP2's performance depends on the volume size, which defines the baseline performance and how quickly it collects I/O credits. Larger volumes have high baseline performance and quick accumulation of

I/O credits. I/O credits denote the available bandwidth GP can use to burst I/O when higher baseline performance is needed. Higher I/O credits signify that it will take more time to burst beyond its baseline performance and the better it functions.

## 2. Provisioned IOPS SSD Volume

One of the fastest and expensive EBS volume that is specifically designed for highly intensive applications like databases. The volume size is around 4 GiB-16TiB and the range of IOPS is a minimum of 100 IOPS and a maximum 32,000 IOPS. In contrast to gp2, io1 uses a consistent IOPS rate when you create volume and so, Amazon EBS delivers the intended IOPS performance.

## 3. Throughput Optimized HDD Volume (st1)

Throughput optimized HDD is different from other types of EBS volumes. It works in terms of throughput instead of IOPS. The reasonably low-cost magnetic storage is suited for large workloads such as data warehouses, log processing, and big data. It supports data that can be frequently accessed. This volume type is suitable for large workloads that require sequential I/O.

## Burst Performance and Throughput credit

St1 uses the same burst-bucket model as gp2 for performance. The volume size decides the baseline throughput of the volume which is the rate at which the volume gathers credits. Larger volumes will have higher burst throughput and baseline. Higher the credits, longer the burst time.

### 4. Cold HDD (sc1) Volume

Cold HDD is another inexpensive magnetic storage that works in terms of throughput instead of IOPS. It has a lower throughput limit as compared to st1 and is suitable for large, infrequently accessed and sequential workloads such as file servers.

## Burst performance and throughput credits

Sc1 uses the same burst-bucket model as gp2 for performance. The volume size decides the baseline throughput of the volume which is the rate at which the volume gathers credits. Larger volumes will have higher burst throughput and baseline. Higher the credits, longer the burst time.

### 5. Magnetic (standard) Volume

Magnetic volume is an old generation magnetic block of storage that can store data which is infrequently accessed. The volume size is about 1 TiB and it has a throughput of 100 MB/s

## Create an Amazon EBS Volume

In this tutorial, you'll learn how to create an Amazon EBS volume which you can attach to your EC2 instance within the same availability zone. You can either create an encrypted volume or a non-encrypted volume, but encrypted volumes have some limitations that are going to be discussed later.

If you want to create an EBS volume suitable for high-performance storage, you should use a provisioned IOPS SSD and assign it to your instance. You can also use st1 and sc1 volumes for the very same purpose.

## How to create an EBS volume

1. Go to https://console.aws.amazon.com/ec2/ to open the EC2 **console.**
2. Choose the **region** on the navigation bar where you want to create the volume.
3. Now go to elastic block store and click on **volumes.**
4. Select **create volume** and choose the **volume type.**
5. Input the size of the volume.
6. If you've chosen **provisioned IOPS volume,** enter the maximum number of IOPS.
7. Select the **availability zone** where you want to create the volume. Remember that EBS volumes can be assigned to those instances residing within the same availability zone.

8. Finally, go to **create volume**. Once the volume status goes active, you can attach it to an instance.

## Restore an EBS volume for a snapshot

You can easily retrieve an Amazon EBS volume along with data from a snapshot. All you need to have is the snapshot ID and access permissions for it.

Snapshots act as a backup to keep the copies of volumes whenever you recreate a snapshot volume. If you attach the restored volume to an instance, you can reproduce data across the region and do whatever you wish to.

New volumes created from existing snapshots take time to load. This means that you don't have to wait for complete data transfer between Amazon S3 and EBS before the attached instances start accessing the data in the volume. If the instance accesses data that hasn't been loaded, the volume downloads the intended data from S3 and loads it in the background.

## Performance of EBS

As soon as the new EBS volumes are available, they work at maximum performance and don't need any initialization.

Volumes that were restored from snapshots, their storage blocks must be removed from Amazon S3 and added to the volume so you could access it. This will take time as it causes a significant increase in the delay of I/O operations when each block is accessed.

The performance increases once the blocks have been downloaded and attached to the volume. If you want to prevent high latency that affects the overall speed, you can enable fast snapshot restore to make sure that the EBS volumes that are created deliver the maximum performance.

## How to Encrypt EBS

EBS volumes restored from encrypted snapshots are already encrypted. If it's an unencrypted snapshot, you can encrypt the volume easily. Note that encrypted volumes can be attached to only those instances that support EBS encryption.

## How to create an EBS volume from a snapshot

1. Go to the Amazon EC2 console and on the navigation bar, chose the **region** where the snapshot is located.

a. If you want to retrieve the snapshot to a volume in another region, simply copy the snapshot to the new location and then restore it to a volume in that region.

2. Chose **elastic block** in the navigation panel.

3. Click on **create volume** and choose the volume type.

4. Type the snapshot ID or description from where you're restoring the volume.

5. Encrypt the volume by selecting **encrypt this volume**.

6. Type the volume **size**. Make sure that the volume size is greater or equal to the snapshot size.

7. Type the maximum number of IOPS.

8. Chose the **availability zone** in which you want to create the volume.

9. Click on **create volume**. Once you restore the volume from a snapshot, you can assign it to an instance and use it.

## How to attach an EBS volume to an instance

You can only attach an EBS volume to a particular instance that resides in the same availability zone as the volume.

1. Go to the Amazon EC2 console.
2. Click on **EBS, Volumes** on the navigation panel.
3. Select the available volume and proceed to **actions**.
4. For **instance**, type the name of the instance ID and chose the instance from the list.
5. For **device**, type the device name or keep the default name.
6. Click on **attach** and connect the EBS volume to your instance.

## How to Delete an Amazon EBS volume

1. Go to Amazon EC2 console.
2. Click on **volume** on the navigation bar.
3. Select the **volume** which you wish to delete and click on **actions, delete volume**
4. A confirmation box will pop up. Click on **yes, delete.**

## Benefits of Amazon EBS

### 1. High Performance

EBS volumes are best for heavy machine-critical applications such as Oracle, Microsoft products and SAP. They are designed for applications that require higher performance and large workloads like big data and data warehousing.

### 2. User-Friendly

There is no hard and fast rule when speaking of creating, deleting and encrypting EBS volumes. The EBS has all the functionalities to change the storage size and volume type according to your requirements. Thanks to EBS, you can easily take backups of volumes and shift it to another region.

## 3. Secure

EBS volumes can be encrypted to ensure security for data compliance. The encryption is supported by each type of volume. Data, snapshots, and disk on the volume are encrypted only if the volume is encrypted.

## 4. Cost-effective

Amazon EBS provides 4 different types of volumes, each having its corresponding price and features. You've options to tune up and down the volume size, its throughput, and storage.

# Section 4: Introduction to Amazon VPC

- ❖ What is Amazon VPC?
- ❖ Components of Amazon VPC
- ❖ Subnet
- ❖ Supported Platforms
- ❖ Difference between default and non-default VPC
- ❖ Elastic Network Interface
- ❖ Route Table
- ❖ Internet Gateway
- ❖ Elastic IP address
- ❖ VPC endpoint
- ❖ NAT
- ❖ VPC Peering Connection
- ❖ VPC Security
- ❖ About Security Groups
- ❖ NACL
- ❖ VPC Flow Logs
- ❖ How to Create a VPC
- ❖ Connectivity Options
- ❖ Rules to follow before you create a VPC
- ❖ Access Control

❖ Use Cases of VPC

AWS has been working on providing security solutions to the clients because let's face it, data breach is one of the common problems especially when data is being shared amongst people in a cloud platform. AWS makes sure that your data is protected from unauthorized access by introducing VPC that is an isolated network within the cloud

## What is Amazon VPC?

Amazon VPC (Virtual private cloud) is the network layer for Amazon EC2 that allows you to launch AWS resources (instances) into a user-defined virtual network. In a virtual network, you can use any of the services provided by AWS. You've full control over the traffic to and from the instances.

There are types of VPCs - Default VPC and user-defined VPC. In default VPC, it has the latest features of EC2 VPC. On the other hand, user-defined VPC gives you the option to configure it according to your requirements. Subnets created in the user-defined VPC are known as non-default subnets. VPC is designed to provide a great level of security to protect the resources and separate it from other resources. You can set up the network topology according to your requirements. For instance, if you want your resources to be not visible to the public or you want the resources to be accessible through the internet.

To understand VPC, take an example of a traditional network present in a data center that consists of hardware resources, and other logical components. Likewise, Amazon VPC is a software based network that works just like a physical data center and is used to transfer packets across the region in a secured manner.

# Components of Amazon VPC

A VPC is dedicated to your account. It's separate from other VPCs in the cloud. You can add instances, subnets, allocate IP address range for the VPC, and configure routing tables and many more.

Below are the components discussed in detail:

## Subnet

A VPC is stretched across an AWS region. A region encompasses of one or more availability zones. Amazon VPC includes subnets that are used for the purpose of separating resources in a particular region. Note that a subnet can't be extended across multiple availability zones.

A subnet is a division of a larger network into smaller networks or subnets. You can run resources into any specific subnet. A public subnet is suitable for resources that need internet access, while a private subnet won't have access to the internet. Subnets not only logically separate resources but they make your applications fault-tolerant. Resources found in every subnet can communicate with each other using private IP addresses.

## Supported Platforms

When Amazon EC2 was first introduced, it supported a single network platform that was shared amongst users called the EC2-classic. Earlier AWS accounts supported EC2-classic as well as VPC but now, accounts only have the support of VPC. By using VPC, you get the authority to:

❖ Assign private IPv4 addresses to the instances
❖ Assign IPv6 addresses to the instances
❖ Choose multiple addresses for the instances.
❖ Introduce network interfaces and assign it to the instances
❖ Modify the security group membership for the instances.

## Difference between default and non-default VPC

If you have an account that supports the VPC platform, it offers a default VPC which has a default subnet. Using default VPC, if in case you don't specify a subnet when open the instance, it runs into the default VPC.

Despite the types of platform your account supports, you have the privilege to create your VPC and perform configuration as per your needs. This is referred to as non-default VPC. Subnets that you create in non-default and default VPC are known as non-default subnets.

## Elastic Network Interface

EC2 instances available in VPC are attached to a network interface called Elastic Network Interface. An ENI has properties like Mac address, private IPv4 address, IPv6 address, security group, and many others. If you remove an ENI from an EC2 instance, the properties will be removed.

By default, VPC has a network interface that is assigned to the instances and this ENI is called the primary network interface. You can't remove the default ENI from an instance, but you have the option to create and assign as many ENIs as you want to the instances.

## Route Table

VPC controls the flow of traffic in and out of the network but how does it know where to go? This is when the routing table comes into play. A route table has a set of rules or routes that defines where the traffic will go. Every VPC has its default route table also known as the main route table. Each subnet in VPC is allocated with only one route table, however, one route table can be assigned to multiple subnets.

By using route tables, you can decide how you want the flow of data i.e. what data should stay in the VPC and what data should be outside the VPC.

## Internet gateway

You can control how the instances launched into a VPC have access to the resources outside the VPC.

The default VPC has an internet gateway and each default subnet is known as a public subnet. Any instance that you launch into a default subnet has private as well as public IPv4 addresses through which they can communicate with the internet. The internet gateway allows instances to have access to the internet using the Amazon EC2 network edge.

Any instance you load into a non-default subnet has a private IPv4 address but no public IP address unless you change the attribute. The instances can communicate with one another but they don't have any access to the internet. If you want to allow internet access to the instances loaded into a non-default subnet, you can attach an internet gateway and assign an elastic IP address to the instance.

## Elastic IP Address

An Elastic IP address is a combination of public and static IPv4 address that is assigned to one instance or network interface at a time in the VPC. An application dependent on an IP address would use an Elastic IP address rather than a public IP address because it isn't static. When an instance shuts down, the public IP address is lost. Therefore, the Elastic IP address is allocated to the instance or network interface. If you don't need it, you can simply release it otherwise, AWS will charge you on an hourly basis.

## VPC endpoint

A VPC endpoint allows you to communicate with other services provided by AWS without using the World Wide Web, VPN connection or NAT. The communication occurs within the VPC so that the traffic doesn't go out of the network. As of now, end-points are compatible with Amazon S3. An endpoint uses the private IP address of instances to enable connection with other services. There can be more than one endpoint in the VPC. You can route traffic from a particular instance to the AWS service through the endpoint.

## Network Address Translation (NAT)

We know that resources in private subnets can't access the internet. However, they do need to have internet access for downloading software updates. A NAT device is responsible for establishing a connection between the resources in the private subnet and the internet or other services. They can only support IPv4 traffic.

AWS offers a NAT gateway, instance, and a managed device. You will have to choose either one of them depending on the use case.

## VPC peering connection

If you've more than one VPCs in the same AWS region, you can enable communication between two or more VPCs through the VPC peering connection. Instances residing in VPC A can communicate with other instances in VPC B.

## VPC Security

Security is imperative when it comes to the transfer of packets from one network to another. There needs to be a way to secure the traffic that enters and leaves your VPC.

To make the VPC more secure, AWS provides add-ons like security groups, VPC, ACL, etc to ensure easy monitoring and security. The routing table is also used for the very same purpose.

## About Security groups

A security group act as a virtual firewall that controls the inbound and outbound traffic for all the instances in VPC. Every VPC has its security group. If you load an instance without specifying a security group, AWS will automatically assign a security group with the instance by default. Each instance can have up to 5 security groups.

To control the flow of traffic, a clear set of rules need to be defined for a security group. Note that the rules should have only permissive rules.

By default, when you create a new security group, it doesn't allow ingress traffic so you've to create a rule that permits inbound traffic. Once you create a rule for inbound traffic, you don't have to create a separate rule for outbound traffics as well since the rule will permit both. The rules can be modified and you can easily add, change or delete a security group.

An ENI can be assigned to 5 security groups whereas, a security group can be attributed to multiple instances. The instances can't, however, communicate with one another except that you set the rule that allows you to do so.

## Network Access Control List (NACL)

In addition to security groups, the network access control list (NACL) is also another virtual firewall that controls the ingress and egress traffic for the subnets present in the VPC. Within a subnet, all instances will follow the same rules. A system administrator of the organization can configure the settings.

By default, Every VPC has NACL that allows all ingress and egress traffic. However, when you create a custom NACL, it doesn't allow any sort of traffic. A subnet that isn't associated with an NACL explicitly will have NACL by default.

To configure traffic, NACL uses the same rules as that of security groups. However, the fine line between the two is that NACL allows you to create allow as well as deny rules.

One NACL can be attached to multiple subnets but each subnet can only have one NACL. The rules are read from lower to a higher number - the highest being 32776. It's advised to create rules in multiples of 100 so you can add more rules easily when needed.

## VPC flow logs

VPC flow is an effective tool that monitors the flow of traffic. It checks whether the traffic is going where it's supposed to go and is received from the desired resources. If any troubleshooting related to traffic occurs, VPC flow logs can easily identify and display it.

You can create a VPC flow log for VPC, subnet or network interface. Resources will be monitored for each component. It will take around 15 minutes to gather data once you've created a flow log.

Every network interface has a different log stream added to a log group in AWS cloud watch logs. You can add multiple logs to the log group. A log contains information about the traffic for a particular resource. You can configure the nature of traffic you want to examine whether it's accepted or rejected traffic. You can give any name to this log in cloudwatch logs and select the resource you want to monitor. You can create flow logs for network interfaces produced by other AWS services like AWS workspace, RDS and many others.

These services itself can't create flow logs, instead use Amazon EC2 to create flow logs. You can delete the log whenever you want to. It will take a few minutes before the removed flow log stops gathering data. There are limitations to the VPC flow log. You can't do any modification after you've created the flow log. Moreover, you can't create VPC flow logs for peered VPCs that don't exist in your AWS account.

## How to create a VPC

We will use the IPv4 Classless Inter-Domain Routing block to create a VPC. There will be two subnet - private and public. To make a private subnet accessible to the internet, a NAT gateway will be used. Furthermore, the VPC will have security groups, as well as ACL, configured to allow inbound and outbound traffic. Follow the steps below:

1. Create a VPC having /16 as its subnet mask and IPv4 CIDR block such as 10.0.0.0/16
2. Create an internet gateway and allocate it to this VPC

3. Create a public subnet having /24 as its subnet mask and IPv4 CIDR block such as 10.0.0.0/24.

4. Create another private subnet having /24 IPv4 CIDR block such as 10.0.1.0/24. Note that the CIDR block must be a subset of a VPC CIDR block and shouldn't be the same as the CIDR block of a public subnet.

5. Generate a custom route table and create a path for all the traffic going to the internet via the gateway. Assign this route table with the public subnet.

6. Create a NAT gateway and attach it to the public subnet. Allot Elastic IP address (EIP) to the NAT gateway.

7. Repeat step 6 for the private subnet.

8. Create a network ACL for the subnets and add rules that will define inbound and outbound traffic.

9. Generate security groups for instances to be stored in public and private subnets. Devise the rules for these security groups and assign them with instances.

10. Create one instance in public and private subnet both. Allocate a security group to each of the instances. An instance in a public subnet must have a public EIP or IP address.

11. Check that the public instances can access the internet while the private instances can have access to the internet through NAT.

Once you've successfully created a VPC, you'll see the following architecture as shown below. You can see that the private subnet has database servers as its instances whereas the public subnet has web servers. The NAT gateway must have EIP to forward traffic to the internet gateway as the source IP address. This architecture shows that the public and private subnet resides in one availability zone, however, it's very much possible to have a similar configuration for additional availability zones.

## Connectivity options

There are three connectivity options offered by AWS VPC that offer safe connection to the VPC, which are as follows:

### 1. Connecting User Network to AWS VPC

You can add resources in your remote network such as computing power, monitoring etc so that the user can have easy access to the resources available in AWS VPC. For using this connection, make sure that you've non-overlapping IP ranges for networks on the cloud to ensure that there is a separate CIDR block for the VPC.

You can connect the user network to AWS VPC by configuring AWS customer VPN gateway using encrypted hardware VPN connectivity. You're charged for every hour the VPC connection is running, and for data transfer.

You can configure the settings by using the existing internet connection or you could use a dedicated connection offered by AWS. One side of the cable is connected to your router while the other end to the AWS router. The speed of the internet connection does affect the performance but with AWS dedicated internet connection, you can get seamless network performance with low bandwidth cost.

If you've multiple remote networks, you will need VPN connections for every remote network. You can use a VPN cloud hub that provides safe and secure communication between the networks. You can create a virtual private gateway for your VPC with customer gateways for the remote networks in order to use cloudhub.

### 2. Peer to Peer connection

If you want to connect multiple AWS VPCs, you can achieve it using the VPC peering option. The resources can communicate with one another using private IP addresses. However, the VPCs needs to be in the same region.

What if the VPCs are scattered in different regions? How can you access all of the resources? Simply by creating a VPC in each region and peering it with your VPC.

If you have a centralized VPC that has confidential information, you can configure which VPC can have access to it. For example, an organization wants to access private records, the organization can peer their VPC with the centralized VPC to access the resources. AWS also charges for VPC peering connection.

## Rules to follow before you create VPC

By following these top practices as suggested by AWS, you can integrate your resources (data, applications, etc) in VPC and keep it fully secured.

### 1. Plan before you create a VPC

It's important to take some time out to plan out the design of the architecture for the VPC. A poor VPC design hurts the availability, flexibility, and security of the structure.

Think of the objective of creating a VPC. Identify the number of subnets you need and what connections you'll need to connect remote networks.

### 2. Decide the CIDR block

A VPC has a CIDR block ranging from 16 to 28 which would determine the number of IP addresses for your VPC. Once you've created a VPC with a CIDR block, you can't modify it. You'll need to create another VPC and transfer your resources to the new VPC if you want to change the CIDR block. It's feasible to choose /16 CIDR block for the VPC so that you won't be ever short of IP addresses when you increase the number of instances.

### 3. Must have Unique range of IP address

Whether it's internal, external, data centers, networks on cloud and other AWS services, make sure you've defined unique IP addresses for all the environments. Before you create a VPC, make sure it doesn't conflict with any other network that you wish to connect with.

### 4. Don't change the Default VPC

AWS sets the default VPC settings for your account. It's advised to leave the default VPC alone since it has all the components linked with it such as subnets, networks, security groups, etc and has the default configuration. Begin with creating a custom VPC using a VPC wizard in the AWS console or CLI. You can configure the settings as per your needs.

If a subnet isn't linked with any route table or NACL, it's linked to the default NACL settings and main routing table. Don't change the main route table because doing that will give paths to other subnets.

### 5. Design according to region expansion

Periodically, AWS adds more availability zones. We know that a subnet is limited to one availability zone. Therefore, it's important to reserve IP addresses for future purposes to expand when you're creating subnets that are a subset of the CIDR block.

### 6. Architecture Tiers

Design your subnets according to the architecture tiers like database tier, business tier, and an application tier. Moreover, you should create subnets in multiple availability zones so that the application is more fault-tolerant. Each subnet in every availability zone should have equally sized subnets and each of the subnets must use a routing table especially designed for them.

## 7. Secure your resources in the private subnet

To secure your resources and VPC, keep your resources in a private subnet. If you want the resources to access the internet, you can add Elastic Load Balancer (ELB) in the public subnet and insert all instances using ELB in the private subnet.

You can also use a NAT gateway that allows instances in the private subnet to use the internet securely.

## 8. Security groups versus NACLs

Both of them are security firewalls that define rules to secure your subnets and resources. It's easier to configure security groups as compared to NACL because the settings of NACL isn't changed frequently. It's the main security policy of the organization and it becomes difficult to manage the NACL rules as they are tied to the IP address.

On the other hand, security groups are linked to instances, and the rules can be expanded in the entire VPC. They are simple and easy to manage.

## Access Control

When you're creating a VPC, you need to configure IAM roles for each instance so that authorized users can only access the resources as there can be more than one user who could manage the resources. Therefore, allocate permissions to those who can have access based on their roles.

## Use VPC Peering

When you're connecting two VPCs using the VPC peering option, instances in the VPCs can communicate with one another using a private IP address. AWS uses its internal network for a VPC peering connection so you don't have to use an external network as it's less reliable and secure.

## Elastic IP versus Public IP

The advantage of using Elastic IP over Public IP is that they can be assigned to any instances, regardless of whether they are running or not. It can persist without an instance. Moreover, the EIP can be moved to the Elastic Network Interface. When you disassociate a public IP address from the instance, you can't use it anymore.

However, an Elastic IP can reused as it has the quality of being persistent.

## Tags

It's a good practice to tag an instance once it's created. You can include tags like version, team, cost, owner, etc.

## Use Cases of VPC

### 1. Hosting a Website

You can host any website such as a blog or any other simple website using VPC. All you've to do is create a public subnet using the VPC console and choose the single public subnet option. To secure your website, you can use NACL or security groups to restrict outbound traffic.

### 2. Hosting a web-based application

VPC is a good solution for hosting a web-based application since it has built-in services like database server, web server and other essential components needed for a website.

For example, you create a public subnet that has web and application servers. These two instances would require inbound and outbound access for the traffic. The public subnet will also need a NAT gateway to allow traffic for database resources in the private subnet. The instances in the private subnet can't access the internet. They only communicate with instances in the public subnet.

# Section 5: Elastic Load Balancing

- ❖ Introduction
- ❖ What is AWS Elastic Load Balancer?
- ❖ How does an ELB work?
- ❖ Types of Elastic Load Balancer
- ❖ Using ELB for Host-based Routing
- ❖ Using ELB for path-based Routing
- ❖ Cross zone load balancing
- ❖ Request Routing
- ❖ Routing Algorithm
- ❖ Security in Elastic Load Balancing
- ❖ IAM for Elastic Load Balancing
- ❖ Getting Started with Load Balancer

## Introduction

It's important to distribute workloads across multiple regions to increase the availability and make your applications more fault-tolerant. For this purpose, Amazon has introduced a service called Elastic load balancer to distribute the workload across multiple servers. Furthermore, when your resources increase, it becomes difficult to monitor and manage multiple resources. This is where AWS

Cloudwatch comes into play. In this section, we'll learn about AWS Elastic Load Balancer and Cloudwatch in detail.

## What is AWS Elastic Load Balancer (ELB)

AWS Elastic load balancing is a built service that uniformly distributes workloads and network traffic across resources like virtual servers to decrease application failure and make them easily available. You can add or remove resources from the load balancer whenever your needs change.

## How does an ELB work?

The working of AWS ELB is very simple. The elastic load balancer receives incoming traffic from the clients and routes to their respective destinations. It also checks whether the target that the client wishes to achieve is safe or not. If the ELB finds it suspicious, then it won't proceed and move to other requests of the clients.

To make ELB accept the incoming traffic, you'll have to specify listener(s) in the settings. A listener checks for connection requests. It can be configured using a protocol and port number for the connection requests from the clients to the load balancer. Similarly, the load balancer also uses the protocol and port number for connections from the load balancer to instances.

## Types of Elastic Load Balancers (ELB)

There are three types of load balancers provided by AWS: Classic load balancer, network load balancer, and application load balancer. Each type of load balancer has a unique configuration.

In classic load balancer, instances should be registered with the load balancer whereas, with network load balancers and application load balancers, you register the instances in instance groups.

## Classic Load Balancer

In a classic load balancer, traffic is distributed across EC2 instances in various availability zones. It will route traffic to every single registered target. The routing decisions are taken in either the transport layer or the application layer. You can configure health checks, which are used to closely monitor the health of registered targets so that the classic load balancer can send requests to the healthy instances. To check whether the registered instances can handle the request load or not in each availability zone, it's wise to keep the same number of instances in every availability zone registered with the classic load balance.

## Network Load Balancer

A Network load balancer works at the fourth layer i.e the transport layer of the OSI model. It can process millions of requests per second. Once it receives a connection request, it chooses a target from the target group and then, invokes a TCP connection to the chosen target on the port number specified in the listener's setting.

When you enable an availability zone, the elastic load balancer creates a node in the zone and by default, it carries the traffic over the registered targets in the availability zone. If you activate the option of the cross-zone load balancing, it will distribute traffic across the registered targets in all availability zones.

## Application Load Balancer

An Application load balancer works at the seventh layer i.e the application layer of the OSI model. The ALB receives the requests from the users, checks the packet, selects the best possible target for the packet and sends it.

The components of the application load balancer are as follows:

1. **Listener**

Listener checks for any connection requests from the users by using the protocol and port number that you specify in its configuration. The rules defined for a listener decides how the load balancer is going to route requests to the registered targets. Each rule consists of a priority or condition. When the conditions are fulfilled, actions are executed. You can define a rule for the listener by default.

## 2. Target group

The target group provides a pathway for the requests to the registered targets. You can easily register a target with many target groups.

## 3. Routing Algorithm

You can decide the routing algorithm of your choice. By default, Round Robin is used as the routing algorithm.

# Using ELB for host-based routing

Let's say you've two websites that are hosted in different EC2 instances and you want to broadcast the incoming traffic between the two. If you use Classic Load Balancing, you'll have to create two AWS load balancers but if you switch to the Application load balancer, you will need only one load balancer.

# Using ALB for path-based routing

This type of routing checks the URL path of the websites hosted on EC2 instances. If you want to enable routing between the two URLs, you can use path-based routing.

# Cross Zone Load Balancing

In cross-zone load balancing, the nodes present in a load balancer are responsible for the circulation of requests from clients to the registered instances. When you enable cross-zone load balancing, the load balancer loads allows traffic to flow across the instances in all of the availability zones.

If you disable cross-zone load balancing, the nodes will promote traffic amongst the registered instances only in certain availability zones. In ALB, the cross load balancing is enabled while in NLB the option is disabled.

## Request Routing

The load balancer resolves its domain name using a DNS server before a request is sent by a client to the load balancer. The DNS entry is under the control of Amazon since the load balancers have the domain name "amazonaws.com" The Amazon DNS server provides IP addresses to the client. The IP addresses refer to the load balancer node's address for the load balancer.

For each activated availability zone, ELB creates a network interface with network load balancers. All the nodes residing in the availability zone can use the network interface to obtain a static IP address. You can also allocate an Elastic IP address to each network interface when you're creating the load balancer. With varying application traffic, ELB can scale the load and update the DNS entry.

## Routing Algorithm

Each type of load balancer uses unique routing algorithms. For Application load balancers, the load balancer node that receives the incoming request uses the following method:

a. Firstly, it checks the listener's rules in a certain order to decide which rule to use.

b. Chooses a target from the target group using the routing algorithm that is configured. For each target group, routing is independently performed.

In the case of network load balancers, the following method is followed:

A target is chosen from the target group using the hash flow algorithm. The algorithm works on the following principles:

- ❖ Protocol
- ❖ Source Port and IP address
- ❖ Destination Port and IP address
- ❖ TCP sequence number

**Routes each TCP connection to a single target.**

Lastly, the classic load balancer uses the round-robin routing algorithm for listeners and uses the least outstanding requests for HTTP and HTTPS listeners.

## Security in Elastic Load Balancing

Security is a crucial aspect of AWS that shouldn't be neglected. Amazon makes sure to provide a safe and secure cloud environment for the organizations whose business depends on the data stored in the data centers.

Security is a shared responsibility between AWS and end-users. Two things fall under the shared responsibility model: Security of the cloud and security in the cloud.

### 1. Security of the cloud

Amazon holds the responsibility of providing a fully secure infrastructure to run AWS services in the cloud platform. Not only that, the services are safe to use as the auditors frequently test and analyze security.

### 2. Security in the cloud

The end-user also plays a vital role when it comes to security. You hold responsibility for the sensitive data you store, whether you follow the company's requirements and the rules and regulations.

Elastic load balancing complies with the AWS shared responsibility model, which includes a set of rules and regulations for data integrity and security.

AWS has control over the infrastructure and the data hosted on the infrastructure including the configurations. The users are responsible for the sensitive data they store in the cloud.

To protect your data, it's recommended to create individual user accounts with AWS IAM, so that each user is entitled to perform their job.

If you enable server-side encryption using Amazon S3 encryption keys for ELB access logs, ELB instantly encrypts each access log and stores it in your S3 bucket. It also decrypts the access log files whenever you access them. Each file is encrypted with a unique key, which is also encrypted with a master key.

Aside from that, Elastic Load balancing makes the process of building secure web-based applications much simpler by ending the HTTPS and TLS traffic from the end-users at the load balancer. The load balancer does the work of encryption and decryption.

When you're configuring a listener, you select the cipher algorithm and protocol versions supported by your application and a server certificate to install. AWS certificate manager can be used to manage server certificates.

## IAM for Elastic load balancing

To identify a particular user, AWS uses security credentials to give you access to your resources. When you're using IAM, you've got the privilege to allow users and applications to access the AWS resources either completely, or limited.

By default, IAM users don't have the permission to create, edit or view the resources. To allow a user to gain access to resources like a load balancer, you've to create an IAM policy that permits users to use resources and API actions whenever they need. Once the policy has been created, it's to be attached to the IAM user or the group where the user belongs to.

When you're attaching a policy to a user or group, it either allows or denies the users to have access to do certain tasks on the resources.

For instance, you can create users and groups using IAM. An IAM user could be a system, application or any person. You can grant permission to the users and groups so they could perform actions on the resources.

## Getting Started With Load Balancer

Now that you're familiar with the AWS Elastic load balancer, it's time to create an ELB using the AWS management console. In this tutorial, you'll learn how to create an Application, Classic and Network load balancer.

## How to create an application load balancer

1.  Open up the Amazon EC2 console

2.  Choose a region for the load balancer. Make sure that the region you select is the same you selected for EC2 instances.

3.  Go to navigation panel, click on load balancers under load balancing.

4.  Go to create the load balancer

5.  Choose the type of load balancer. In this example, we've chosen an application load balancer. Proceed to continue.

6.  Configure the load balancer:

    a.  In the name field, type a name for the load balancer

    b.  b. Chose the scheme.

    c.  Choose either IP v4 or IP v6 for IP address type.

    d.  Configure the listener settings. By default, the listener accepts HTTP protocol with port no 80. You can change the settings according to your requirements.

    e.  In the VPC field, choose the same VPC used for your instances on which you want to run your services.

f. . As for the availability zone, tick the checkbox of the availability zone for the load balancer.

7. Go to next: configure security groups.

## How to configure security groups

You've to assign a security group to your load balancer that will allow traffic to the ports that you've mentioned for the listeners.

1. Go to create a new security group on the assign security group page.
2. Type the name and description for your security group.
3. Click on next. You'll be directed to configure routing page.

## How to configure Routing

1. On the configure routing page, fill in the fields:

   a. Type the name of the new target group.

   b. Set the protocol and port number

   c. Choose the target type.

   d. Keep the default health check settings.

2. Proceed to next and you'll be directed to register targets page.

## How to register targets

The load balancer does the job of directing the traffic between the targets that are linked with its target groups. When you connect a target group to an ECS service, Amazon ECS handles the registration automatically by registering or de-registering the container instances with your target group. You don't have to add targets to the target group for this time.

Skip the target registration and go to next. Review your load balancer and then finally click on create your load balancer.

## How to create a classic load balancer

1. Go to Amazon EC2 console.

2. Choose a region for the load balancer. Make sure that the region you select is the same you selected for EC2 instances.

3. Go to navigation panel, click on load balancers under load balancing.

4. Go to create the load balancer

5. Choose the Classic load balancer as the load balancer type.

6. Specify the name of the load balancer.

7. Chose the same network where the container instances are located in a VPC or EC-2 classic.

8.  Configure the listener settings.

9.  Choose a minimum of two subnets in various availability zones. The subnets you chose are moved to the selected subnets box.

10. Go to next to assign security groups.

## How to assign security to your load balancer

If you've created a load balancer in a specific VPC, you've to associate it with a security group that would allow traffic to the ports you specify for the load balancer as well as the health checks. Note that Amazon EC2 doesn't automatically renew the security groups linked with ELB.

## How to configure security groups

1.  Go to create a new security group on the assign security group page.
2.  Type the name and description for your security group.
3.  Click on next. You'll be directed to configure security settings.

## How to configure security settings

1. Go to next to configure health checks for the instances. If ELB comes across an unhealthy task, it will stop forwarding the traffic to the instance hosting that particular task and transmits the traffic to other healthy instances.

On the health check tab, do the following settings:

a. Leave ping protocol to its default value of HTTP

b. Leave ping sort to its default value of 80

c. In the ping path field, change the default value with a forward slash "/". This tells ELB to send health check queries to the web home pages for the webserver.

d. Leave the rest of the fields to its default values.

2. Go to next: Add EC2 instances.

## EC2 Instance Registration

The load balancer does the job of directing the traffic between the instances that are registered to the load balancer. When you connect load balancer to Amazon ECS, Amazon ECS handles the registration automatically by registering or de-registering the container instances when tasks are running on them. You don't have to add container instances to the load balancer.

1. On the add EC2 instances, make sure no instances are selected for registration.
2. Leave the rest of the fields to its default values.
3. Proceed with next. You'll be prompted to add tags.

## How to tag your load balancer

1. Type a key and value for the tag

2.  If you want to add another tag, go to create tag and specify its key and value.

3.  Once you're done adding tags, go to review and create.

## How to create and verify your load balancer

1.  If you want to change any setting, go to edit.

2.  Click on create to create your load balancer.

3.  You'll be notified once your load balancer is successfully created.

# Section 6: Introduction to Amazon CloudWatch

- ❖ What is Amazon Cloud Watch?
- ❖ How does Amazon Cloud Watch work?
- ❖ Components of CloudWatch

Amazon Cloudwatch is one of the commonly used services provided by Amazon that keeps a check on AWS applications and resources on the AWS cloud.

## What is Amazon Cloud Watch?

Amazon Cloud Watch is a management service designed to monitor the resources and applications you use by collecting metrics/logs which are variables that defines the performance measure.

On the Cloudwatch homepage, the metrics are displayed for every AWS service you use. You can also create a custom dashboard that shows metrics of your custom applications. This service is beneficial for developers, IT managers, and engineers as it makes it easier to do diagnostics and troubleshooting to ensure applications are working seamlessly.

You have the option to create alarms that notifies you whenever there are changes made to the resources you're monitoring when a threshold is compromised. For instance, you can check the CPU usage status, and using this information will help you in deciding whether you should load additional resources or not. You can use 10 custom metrics and alarms for free. You'll be charged for additional metrics.

## How does Amazon Cloud watch work?

Amazon Cloudwatch follows a sequence of actions - first, it collects logs and data, then it closely monitors the applications in realtime and acts according to the rules and then, in the end, it analyzes the metrics for further use. During the collection of data, Amazon Cloudwatch continuously monitors and updates the logs. If in case any issues are found, troubleshooting is started.

To put it simply, the service is like a repository of metrics and you can retrieve statistics and visual analysis based on those metrics.

The computing of resources is done in powerful and huge data centers. To ensure flexibility and scalability, each and every data center is located in different regions and each region is separate from other regions so as to achieve stability and prevent system failure. Metrics are also stored in each region so you could analyze the statistics of working in each region.

# Components of CloudWatch

## 1. Namespaces

A namespace is like a container to hold metrics. Metrics found in different namespaces are treated separately so that there is no overlapping.

When you're creating a metric, you specify a namespace that must have valid characters (alphanumeric, underscore, slash, hash, etc.) The AWS namespace follows a typical name convention such as AWS/example.

## 2. Metrics

Metric is the major component in CloudWatch. It corresponds to a variable that is monitored and the values of a variable represent the data points.

You can view the built-in metrics provided by AWS or you can send your custom-made metrics to cloud watch. Metrics only exists in the region in which they are made. They can be deleted, however, they expire after 15 months if there are no data points. You can define a metric by name or namespace.

## 3. Time Stamp

Timestamp refers to date and time that is associated with a metric data point. If you don't create a time stamp, CloudWatch automatically sets up the time stamp based on when the data point was received. The timestamp shows the complete date, hours, minutes and seconds.

## 4. Dimension

A dimension refers to the characteristics that describe a metric. It's a name-value pair that uniquely identifies a metric. You can add up to 10 dimensions to a metric. Dimensions make it easier to locate a certain metric and obtain its statistics. For instance, if you want to get statistics for a particular EC2 instance, you can specify the dimension for the instanceID.

There are some metrics generated by other AWS services such as Amazon EC2 for which CloudWatch can aggregate data and display the statistics. If you're searching for metrics in the AWS/EC2 namespace but don't mention any dimensions, CloudWatch will aggregate all of the data for the mentioned metric and output the statistics.

## 5. Statistics

Cloudwatch provides data aggregation over a specific period. Data aggregation is the collection of related things altogether and it's computed by using the metric name, dimension, namespace, and data point.

AWS provides a list of available statistics as mentioned below:

### 6. Minimum

It's the lowest value that is observed during the specified period.

### 7. Maximum

It's the maximum or highest value that is observed during the specified period.

### 8. Sum

Values belonging to the same metric are added together. This statistic helps determine the total volume of a metric.

### 9. Average

It's the ratio of sum and sample count during the specified period. By comparing the value of average to Minimum and Maximum, it will help you in deciding when to increase or decrease the resources.

### 10. Sample count

It records the number of data points.

### 11. pNN.NN

It's the value of the specified percentile. Using up to 2 decimal places, you can type any percentile.

# Units

Each statistic is measured in units which could be seconds, percent, bytes, etc. Whenever you create a custom-made metric, it's a good practice to specify the unit. If you don't mention any unit, Cloud watch uses none as the unit. By specifying units, you make the data more meaningful. Cloud watch will aggregate similar data having the same units and output the results. If you don't specify a unit, Cloud watch will treat all the data same.

# Period

A period refers to the time duration associated with a statistic. Each statistic shows data aggregation over a specific time frame. It's measured in seconds and the valid values for period are multiples of 60.

If you want to retrieve statistics of any metric, you can mention parameters like start time, end time and period. These variables return the overall length of time of the corresponding statistics. The default values of the parameters will output a collective set of statistics of the previous hour.

When you aggregate the statistics over a time frame, they are marked with time corresponding to the starting time. For example, data aggregated from 10:00 pm-11:00pm is marked as 10:00pm.

Furthermore, data aggregated between 10:00 pm – 11:00pm becomes visible at 10:00pm. The aggregated data may change as more samples are being collected during the time duration.

Periods can be used for alarms. When you want to monitor a metric, the cloud watch compares the metric to the threshold value that a user specifies. You can specify the time over which the comparison takes place, and you can mention how many evaluation periods are needed to reach to the conclusion.

## Aggregation

Statistics can be aggregated on the basis of period you specify when you're retrieving statistics. You're allowed to add data points having similar time period so that AWS CloudWatch can aggregate them. CloudWatch doesn't aggregate data according to the region.

Not only you can aggregate data according to the period, but you can do the same for dimensions and namespace. You can add data points for same or different metrics, with different time frames.

In a distributed system, metrics from different sources having same dimensions and namespaces are treated as a single metric.

## Percentile

A percentile tells the position of a value in a dataset. Now you might be wondering why and where percentiles are used? Whenever you're running a website or an application, you need to make sure if it's running to its maximum potential to provide a greater user experience. When you're looking at the averages, you may not be able to see the big picture because the average may not include the outliers, for example, that 5% of the users didn't have a good experience.

Percentiles are indeed a useful statistic that helps you to understand the behavior and performance of the application you're running. Some CloudWatch metrics support the use of percentiles. You can specify the percentile up to 2 decimal places and use it when creating an alarm.

Percentile is available for custom metric as well provided that you publish the un-summarized data point. However, you can't use it for metric values, which are negative.

## Alarm

An alarm is used to invoke actions automatically. It can watch a single metric over a specific period and performs an action based on the metric value against the threshold value.

The action is a notification that is sent to Amazon SNS or Auto scaling policy. There is an option to add an alarm on the dashboard.

When you're creating an alarm, select a period greater or equal to the frequency of the metric that is monitored. For example, detailed monitoring provides metrics for your EC2 instances every 1 minute. This means that you need to set an alarm of 1 minute (60 seconds).

# Section 7: AWS Database Services

- ❖ Introduction to Amazon Database Services
- ❖ Why should you use AWS database?
- ❖ Types of AWS database services
- ❖ Introduction to Amazon Relational Database Service
- ❖ Database Instances
- ❖ Multi A-Z deployment of Amazon RDS
- ❖ Database Engines
- ❖ How to create an RDS Instance
- ❖ How to delete a DB instance
- ❖ Introduction to Amazon Redshift
- ❖ How does Amazon Redshift works?
- ❖ Performance
- ❖ How to set up Amazon Redshift
- ❖ Introduction to DynamoDB
- ❖ Terminologies
- ❖ DynamoDB API
- ❖ Naming Conventions
- ❖ Data types
- ❖ Amazon DynamoDB Partitions

# Introduction to Amazon Database Services

The term "database" must be familiar to all of you. It's a container of storing data that is maintained and retrieved. Database systems have become an integral part of large-scale organizations whose business depends on data. Therefore, it's essential to have a database service that stores, manages, retrieves, as well as protect data. Amazon introduced a list of database services that helps you to deploy a cloud-based database with ease without having to put extra effort in maintaining the database.

## Why should you use AWS Database?

Earlier when cloud databases weren't introduced, organizations used conventional in-house database systems that were continuously monitored and maintained, 24/7, in case of any performance issues. The database management team was hired who would take care of the hardware requirements, install security patches and release new software to make the application more effective. This not only made the task more time consuming but also became a hassle to manage the entire system.

Thanks to AWS database services who took care of the problems once and for all. Users only have to take care of the application layer and expanding their business, while the rest is handled by AWS at absolutely no cost.

## Types of AWS database services

AWS offers a wide spectrum of relational and non-relational databases designed to cater to the user's requirements. For any database requirement, you'll find the database service you need. You can build your database from scratch or import an already existing Oracle, Microsoft SQL, and MySQL database engines.

The different types of databases provided by the AWS are as follows:

### 1. Relational Database

In RD, the data is collected in a tabular format. It uses structured query language (SQL) to perform operations like insertion, deletion, updating, editing and many more. AWS offers Amazon RDS, Amazon Redshift and Amazon Aurora which are relational database services.

### 2. In-memory database

In-memory databases store data in main memory such as RAM. Whenever you want to access the data, you'll have to go to your main memory instead of the hard disk. We know that primary storage is faster than secondary storage and this is what makes In-memory databases so popular. Amazon ElastiCache is one example of the service.

### 3. Key-value database

A key-value database is a non-relational database that uses the key-value approach to store data. The key is a unique identifier attached to data so if you want to search for a particular piece of data, the key will locate it for you. Amazon Dynamo DB is a key-value database offered by AWS.

# Introduction to Amazon RDS (Relational Database Service)

Amazon RDS is a database service that allows you to set up an easy, cost-effective and secure relational database system that is connected via the internet. It eliminates the monotonous tasks by managing common administrative tasks. With Amazon RDS, you can manage your resources like memory, storage, and CPU and scale them as per your needs. In case of failures, it's important to have a backup of the data. Amazon RDS provides the facility of automated backups so you can retrieve it for future use. What's great about this service is that it's compatible with famous database engines like SQL Server, MYSQL, Oracle and many others. Just as keeping backup of the data is important, similarly, security is a crucial factor. By using AWS identity and access management, you have control over who can access the database and who can't. You can protect your databases in a virtual cloud environment.

## Database Instances

A Database instance is an isolated database system in the cloud that can have multiple databases created by users. To create and edit a database instance, you can use the AWS management console or CLI. Each instance works on a particular database engine and AWS support the use of MariaDB, Oracle, MySQL and many other. Every engine has its unique features.

There are 3 different types of DB instance storage: General purpose, Magnetic and Provisioned IOPS. They differ in their performances and price. Depending on the storage type and data engine it uses, each instance has a minimum and maximum storage needs. Sufficient storage allows databases to expand and use the features of DB engines.

One can run a DB instance by using the Amazon virtual private cloud. When you're using a virtual private cloud, you've got the choice to create subnets, configure routing, choose IP address range, etc. The operation of Amazon RDS is the same regardless of any environment.

## Multi-AZ deployment of Amazon RDS

In case of any failure, Amazon RDS provides the facility of replicating the primary DB instance across various availability zones to reduce latency rate, resume database operations and solve I/O problems. The copy of the primary database instance is known as a standby replica. What if you wish to have a read-only copy of the database? You can create a read replica by specifying the database as the source and then Amazon RDS takes a snapshot to create a read-only copy of the database. Make sure that the source DB has automatic backups enabled before you set up the read replica option.

## Benefits of Using Read Replica in AWS RDS

1. One of the major benefits of using read-replica is that you reduce the load on the source/primary database instance by simply transferring read queries from the source application to the read replica. You can easily scale out a single DB instance for heavy database workloads

2. It's an effective disaster recovery strategy as source DB instances are bound to fail anytime.

## Database Engines

AWS RDS supports six database engines, each of which has its unique features. Even though every RDBS engine does the same job but some factors need to be considered when you're choosing a database engine such as storage requirements, flexibility, feasibility, interoperability, and how secure the database engine is.

### 1. Amazon Aurora

Amazon Aurora is a relational database service that is easy to use and cost-effect. It's nothing less than a high-end commercial database. It offers greater performance than MySQL and PostgreSQL. Aurora supports all versions of MySQL and PostgreSQL. This means the tools, features, and drivers all are available in Amazon Aurora. Here's why you should use the database service:

❖ **Secure**

The DB service is completely secure. You can isolate your database instance by using Amazon VPC and use encryption keys to protect your data from being accessed by unauthorized users.

❖ **Scalable**

There is an auto scaling feature, which means whenever you feel the need to increase the number of resources such as storage, you can do so. You don't have to manually increase the storage space. Amazon Aurora does the job for you.

❖ **Durable**

You can replicate the source database across multiple regions so you don't have to worry about database failure.

❖ **Easy Management**

Amazon Aurora offers easy management. You can set up the database instance with AWS console or CLI. Moreover, you can track the status of your instances using Amazon Cloudwatch for absolutely no cost. From updating to provisioning, everything is under the hands of Amazon Aurora.

## Pricing

Pricing varies according to the region. If you've set North Virginia as your region, the database storage cost is $0.10 GB/per month and the backup storage is $0.021 GB/per month.

## MySQL

MySQL is one of the popular relational database tools, however, its popularity has seen a decline because of the tough competitors in the market. It has got stability issues when speaking of performing functions like auditing, referencing, etc. Moreover, it performs poorly when it handles a large amount of data since large data means there will be a high read/write ratio.

Although the database service isn't designed to work in every situation, it has its upsides when it comes to usage.

# Advantages

❖ **Easy to use**

MySQL is a fairly simple database solution that is easy to install, implement and work on it.

❖ **Inexpensive**

MySQL isn't an expensive database system to work on as compared to other available database engines. The implementation would cost you between free to $10,000.

❖ **Industrial Standard**

MySQL is a commonly used database system that is compatible to work with any operating system and complies with industry standard.

# Pricing

The cost of database storage is around $0.115 GB per month while the cost of backup storage is around $0.095 GB per month.

# MariaDB

MariaDB is another effective RDBMS engine that is similar to MySQL but has various added features. It's purely open-source, meaning that it only uses one single license. Amazon RDS makes it easier to deploy scalable MariaDB databases within minutes. MariaDB versions 10.0-10.3 are supported by Amazon RDS.

# Benefits

### ❖ Availability

You can replicate the database instances to increase the availability and flexibility of the data. The multi-AZ deployment options are available that allows replication of databases across availability zones.

### ❖ Scalable

You can scale up the resources for MariaDB instances up to 244GiB memory and 32 vCPUs. The storage can also be increased.

### ❖ Secure

Amazon RDS gives you the guarantee of the complete security of your databases. Your data can be protected using encryption keys.

### ❖ Automatic backup

By default, Amazon RDS enables the backup option. It keeps backup of your databases and data and allows you to restore it whenever you want to. You can also create DB snapshots that are backups of the DB instances. It gives you the advantage of creating a new instance from a snapshot.

# Pricing

The cost of database storage is $0.115 GB per month whereas the cost of backup storage is $0.095 GB per month.

## SQL Server

Microsoft SQL Server is a relational database management system that was developed by Microsoft. With just a few clicks, you can deploy, operate and scale SQL server in the cloud. Amazon RDS can deploy 2012, 2014, 2016 and 2017 versions of SQL Server in no time.

You don't have to separately buy the licenses for SQL server. The license is included when you purchase the software.

Moreover, there are no upfront fees. You pay on an hourly basis for the services you use. You have the option to purchase reserved DB instances on a one or three-year reservation basis.

## Pricing

The cost of database storage is around $0.115 GB per month and as for backup storage, it's 0.095 GB per month.

**How to create an RDS instance**

1. Sign in to **AWS management console**.
2. Go to **services** and click on **RDS**.
3. Select **create database** and then choose the database engine of your option. In this example, we'll choose MySQL.
4. Tick the only **enable options eligible for the RDS Free Usage Tier** checkbox. Proceed to **next**.
5. Scroll down and specify DB instance identifies, **master user name** and **password**. Click on **next**.

6. In the database options, specify a **database name**.

7. Under the backup section, chose the **backup retention period** and select the number of days that Amazon RDS would retain backups. Untick the copy tags to snapshot checkbox.

8. Check the **enable deletion protection** checkbox.

9. Your database instance has been created. To see the **details**, click on **view DB instance details**.

10. Once the status has turned available, it's time to connect it to the shell.

    a. Click on database, copy the endpoint and paste it in notepad.

    b. Open MySQL shell and copy-paste the details such as username, endpoint, and port number. When you press enter, you'll be asked to provide the password.

11. Check whether the database you created exists or not.

## How to Delete a DB instance

Once you've connected a DB instance to the local server, you have the option to delete it if you no longer wish to use it. Follow the steps below:

1. Log in to the **AWS management console** and open the Amazon RDS console.

2. Chose **databases** in the navigation panel

3. Select the DB instance you wish to delete

4. Select **delete** in the **actions box**

5. Select **no** in the **create final snapshots**

6. Go to **delete.**

# Introduction to Amazon Redshift

Amazon Redshift is the fastest cloud data warehouse that is equipped with powerful data metrics to evaluate your business. From sales to logistics to performance, the platform offers deep insights into every aspect of your business.

It's a petabyte-scale data warehouse that allows you to store and analyze data in the cloud. Those days have long gone now, when businesses had to rely on the traditional approach of forecasting and making predictions. With Redshift, you can perform predictive analysis and concentrate on other parts of the organization. You can customize analytical tools to make better decisions that promote the growth of the business. For large-scale data migrations, Amazon redshift is the optimal solution.

# How does Amazon Redshift Works?

Amazon Redshift connects to machine-learning tools and SQL-based clients via a database. The data warehouse consists of a collection of resources called nodes that are further organized into a group known as a cluster. Each cluster is powered by a Redshift engine and has one or more databases.

You can use Amazon Redshift to improve customer service, enhance the productivity of the business, track the performance and many more.

## Pros

Amazon redshift is an exceptional alternative to its counterparts. It beats the traditional data warehouse in many ways.

### 1. Performance

Amazon Redshift delivers the most breakneck speed on huge data sets having sizes of petabytes and more. Not even traditional data warehouses can beat the speed at which Redshift processes data.

It uses columnar data storage and parallel processing design to provide an enhanced level of performance.

### 2. Scalability

You don't have to worry, ever whether your data size increases or decreases when Amazon Redshift is there for the rescue! In traditional warehouses, you need to purchase costly hardware equipment to meet the needs of the ever-growing data. However, using Redshirts allows flexibility and scalability with just a few clicks. You can scale up or down the number of resources and you only have to pay for what you use.

### 3. Security

The security factor can't be compromised. Therefore, Amazon sets security as a top priority. It follows the shared responsibility model in which Amazon is responsible for providing security of the cloud whereas the organization is responsible for the data that resides in the cloud.

Having said that, Amazon redshift creates cluster security groups and assigns it to data clusters for internal access. Organizations using a VPC can also use the Redshift environment. When you create a cluster, you'll find an option of data encryption as well.

### 4. Cost

Amazon Redshift provides top-notch performance at an affordable cost. The service gives you the freedom from purchasing hardware resources and maintaining it since it's the job of Redshift.

## Cons

### 1. Requires a solid understanding of the functions

Amazon Redshift has distribution keys and sort keys, both of which decides how data can be stored and indexed across nodes. Hence, you need to have a proper understanding of the concepts so you can use them properly.

## 2. Compatibility issues

If you've data in Amazon S3 or Dynamo DB, you can load it to redshift via parallel processing feature. However, for other Amazon services, this feature isn't supported. You'll have to look for alternatives such as scripts to put the data in redshift.

# Performance

Amazon Redshift uses two architectures to deliver the fastest performance - Massive Parallel Processing and Columnar data storage.

# Massive Parallel Processing

MPP distributes the workload across nodes in every cluster, thus speeding up the process of queries operations on huge amounts of data. Multiple nodes can perform the same processing of all the SQL functions in parallel and then they are finally aggregated.

# Columnar Data Storage

Columnar storage makes sure that the I/O requirements are optimal. When the information in the table is stored in a columnar order, the amount of data required to be loaded from disk is reduced and the number of I/O requests is lessened. When there are fewer data loaded into the memory, Redshift can perform more processing on queries.

## How to Set Up Amazon Redshift

Before you set up Redshift, you need to complete the following pre-requisites:

❖ **Account**

You must have an AWS account before you get started with Amazon Redshift

❖ **Firewall Port**

There needs to be an open port that Redshift can use. No matter what the port number is, your connection won't be established if the port isn't open in your firewall.

❖ **Permissions**

If you want Amazon RDS to have an access to other Amazon services such as Amazon S3, you can grant permissions in two ways:

1. By providing the AWS access key to an IAM user having the permissions.

2. By creating an IAM role attached to the redshift cluster.

## How to launch a Redshift Cluster

Once you've completed the prerequisites, it's time to launch a redshift cluster. Follow these steps:

1. Open the Amazon redshift console
2. Choose the **region** in which you want to create the cluster
3. Click on **quick launch cluster** and provide the details such as node type, number of compute nodes, etc.
4. Go to **launch cluster** and wait for some time till the launch finishes. When done, you can return to the list of clusters. You'll see the cluster you made in the list. Make sure the cluster status says available.
5. Click on the cluster you launched and click the **cluster** button. Go to **modify cluster**. Select the **VPC security group** you wish to attach with this cluster and click **modify** to save association.

## How to Connect To the Cluster and Run Queries

After you've launched a cluster, it's time to connect to the cluster and start running the queries.

1. Using the **AWS Query Editor**, connect to the cluster from the AWS management console.
2. Connect to the cluster via a SQL client tool.

## Introduction to DynamoDB

Like other database systems, DynamoDB is a NoSQL database service offered by Amazon. Undoubtedly, the database is the building block for any organization, whether small or large. Traditional databases are no longer the only solution to the problems since every day our requirements change, and the workload increases. Therefore, a database engine like DynamoDB can greatly tackles the challenges of the organizations.

Unlike a relational database, Amazon DynamoDB works on the key-value pair method to add, delete update and retrieve data. A primary key is needed to distinguish the different records of data, but it doesn't need a schema to create a table. DynamoDB provides great performance when you want to scale up the resources.

Three components make up DynamoDB: tables, properties/attributes, and items. A table holds information or items in a tabular form and attributes refer to information about the set of items.

## Terminologies

- ❖ **Table:** A table is a group of records. For example, if you want to store patient records, you'll need Patient ID, Name, Phone, Address and all the relevant details that will be stored in a table.

❖ **Item:** Item refers to an individual record that uniquely defines the entry in the table. For example, a particular patient record is an Item.

❖ **Attribute:** It's a field that is linked to an item such as Patient ID, Name, etc.

❖ **Primary key:** A unique field/attribute that should be created when you're creating a table. For example, patient ID will be set as a primary key since it's unique for every patient.

There are two types of primary key supported by DynamoDB:

**a. Simple Primary Key**

A simple primary key is the same as the general primary key. It's also known as a partition key that refers to only single attribute. For instance, Patient ID in Patient records table.

**b. Composite Primary Key**

On the other hand, a composite primary key is a combination of partition key and sort key. For example, in a car details table, the car model name and model number can be treated as composite primary key.

❖ **Secondary Index**

A secondary index helps you find the record you're looking for without the use of primary key.

You can use secondary indexes to query your data. Once you create a secondary index, you can search the data using the index.

There are two types of indexes supported by DynamoDB:

a. **Global secondary Index:** It's a combination of partition key and sort key different from the table.

b. **Local secondary index**: An index having the same partition key but different sort key as the table.

❖ **Dynamo DB streams**

It's an optional feature that keeps a track of any data changes in the table. For example, whenever you add, modify or delete data, a new event occurs and the event is stored in a stream record.

a. **A new item is added:** The stream record takes an image of the item in the table, including its attributes.

b. **An item is modified:** "before" and "after" image of the modified attributes are captured.

c. **An item is deleted:** The stream captures the entire record before it was deleted.

Each Dynamo DB stream record has the name of the table and other metadata. It has a lifetime of 24 hours; after which it's removed from the stream.

# DynamoDB API

Before you start working with Amazon DynamoDB, you need to be aware of the API operations which are as follows:

# Control Plane

Control Plane compromises of a list of operations for creating and managing a table. You can use the following operations:

1. **CreateTable:** Allows you to create a new table.
2. **DescribeTable:** Gives information about the table such as indexes, primary key, composite key, etc.
3. **UpdateTable:** allows you to change the settings of table, indexes or dynamoDB stream.
4. **DeleteTable:** allows you delete a table.
5. **ListTable:** outputs all of the table names in the list.

# Data Plane

Data plan operations allows you to perform actions on table like read, update and delete.

❖ **Creating Data**

**a. PutItem:** You can write a single item to a table using the primary key.

**b.BatchWriteItem:** allows you to write up to 25 items to a table. This operation also lets you delete multiple items from one or more tables.

❖ **Reading Data**

**a. GetItem:** You can retrieve a particular item using the primary key.

**b. Query:** It retrieves an item which has a partition key.

**c. BatchGetItem:** It can retrieve multiple items from multiple tables.

- **Updating data**

**a. UpdateItem:** You can modify one or more data items using the primary key.

❖ **Deleting Data:**

**a. DeleteItem:** You can delete an item from the table using the primary key.

**b. BatchWriteItem:** It allows you to delete multiple items up to 25 in a table.

## DynamoDB Streams

a. **ListStreams:** it outputs the list of streams
b. **DescribeStream:** It gives information about the stream and the resources used
c. **GetRecords:** returns one or more stream records with the help of given shard iterator.
d. **GetShardIterator:** It returns a shard iterator that is basically a data structure for storing information about the stream.

# Transactions

Transaction helps to maintain the data correctness within and across the tables. You can use the following options:

**a. TransactWriteItems:** It allows put, update and delete operation to multiple data items both within and across tables.

**b. TransactGetItems:** It allows you to retrieve items from one or more tables.

# Naming Conventions

Tables, attributes and other objects should have a name and their names must be meaningful and short such as Patient, Products, etc.

The rules are as follows:

❖ All names should be case-sensitive and encoded using UTF-8
❖ Names and indexes must have characters between 3 and 255 long. They can have the following characters:
❖ Lower case letters a-z
❖ Uppercase letters A-Z
❖ Numeric digits 0-9
❖ underscore
❖ dash
❖ dot

The attribute name must be between 1 and 255 characters long.

## Data Types

Amazon DynamoDB supports different types of data types:

- ❖ **Scalar Types:** The scalar types include string, numeric, binary, Boolean and null values.
- ❖ **Set Types:** The set types can have multiple scalar values.
- ❖ **Document Types:** there are two types of document types - list and map.

## Amazon DynamoDB partitions

## What is a partition?

A partition is a block of storage for a table that is backed up by solid state dives and is automatically replicated across multiple availability zones. When data grows, the number of partition also increases. This is the process that DynamoDB handles.

When you're creating an item, the partition key is transmitted to the hash function of DynamoDB. This hash function finds out in which partition the item will be stored. When you want to search for a particular item, DynamoDB searches the item through its partition key and passes it to the hash function.

## Partition Limit

A single partition can hold a maximum of 10 GB of data which means one partition may have 25,000 items. Despite the size of the data, the partition can support a maximum of 3000 read capacity units and 1000 write capacity units.

## How Partitions Are Created

When you're creating a table, the provisioned capacity of the table calculates how many partitions will be defined. The equation below is used to calculate how many partitions will be created:

(Read capacity units/3000) + (write capacity units/1000) = no of initial partitions.

Suppose, the RCU is 2500 units and WCU is 1000 units, what will be the number of partitions? The answer is two. As soon as the data size becomes greater than the maximum size of the partition, DynamoDB automatically splits a single partition into two.

## How to Create a Table in DynamoDB

1. Log into your AWS account and go to the Amazon DynamoDB console.
2. Click on create table and provide the details such as table name, primary key, etc and proceed to create.
3. You'll be able to see your table. Go to items to insert, edit or add a query to the table.

## How to Insert an Item in DynamoDB

Once you've created a table, it's time to insert items in your table.

1. Go to items and click on create item.

2. A JSON file will be opened. Select the "+" symbol and click on append. You'll see the drop down menu. Choose the type of item you wish to insert.

3. Click on save to save the progress.

## How to Perform Queries in DynamoDB

1. Go to **items** and choose what you wish to filter out.

2. Click on **start search.**

# Section 8: Amazon SQS, SWS and SNS

- ❖ What is the Amazon Simple Queue Service?
- ❖ How does Amazon SQS work?
- ❖ Amazon SQS Dead-letter Queues
- ❖ Benefits of using SQS
- ❖ Cons of Amazon SQS
- ❖ Use Cases of Amazon SQS
- ❖ What is Amazon SWS?
- ❖ Terminologies
- ❖ How does Amazon SWS work?
- ❖ What is Amazon SNS?
- ❖ Terminologies
- ❖ Amazon SNS API
- ❖ Use Cases of Amazon SNS

## What is the Amazon Simple Queue Service?

Amazon SQS is a messaging service introduced by Amazon to administer asynchronous communication between applications or services.

The term "Queuing" in Amazon Simple Queue Service may be confusing to most of you. Take an example of communication between two subscribers via a cellular network. There are two speakers: The sender who sends the message and the recipient who receives the message. If there is direct communication between the two, both users need to be active.

Asynchronous communication is related to the messaging service, however, the main underlying difference is if the recipient is offline at the moment, the message sent by the sender will be on hold in the server. As soon as the receiver is available, the message will be delivered and received by the recipient.

Messages are processed in two ways:

❖ **Standard queues**: It's the default type that can handle multiple messages in any order in the queue. It makes sure that the message is delivered at least once and the duplicates are sent into the queue.

❖ **FIFO queues**: It offers first in first out delivery. The order of the messages is preserved and the message is delivered only once. The message is available to the receiver unless he/she delete it.

# How does Amazon SQS work?

## Message Lifecycle

1. The producer sends a message to a queue and the message becomes redundant as its spread across the Amazon SQS servers.

2. When the recipient is available to receive the message, it consumes the message present in the queue and the message is returned. As the message is being processed, it remains in the queue throughout the visibility period. The visibility timeout is the time frame when the message is secure from receiving and processing by other recipients.

3. The receiver deletes the message from the queue to stop the message from being received and going through the same process again when the time out clock expires.

## Amazon SQS Dead-letter Queues

Amazon SQS supports the dead-letter queue feature in which the message sent by the sender isn't received by the recipient due to issues. This is known as dead-letter queues. They are useful in debugging the application because it lets you identify the problematic messages that were failed to be processed.

Let's say, a user places an order for product, but now the product is no longer available. An error will be generated and the message is sent to the dead-letter queue. Another problem could be that the sender and receiver failed to understand the protocol they use to communicate causing the message to corrupt.

Note that the dead-letter queue of a FIFO queue must be a FIFO queue. Likewise, the dead-letter queue of a standard queue must be a standard queue.

## Benefits of using SQS

The use of Amazon SQS has proven to be beneficial.

### 1. Easy setup

SQS is a managed service for which you don't have to set up the infrastructure. All you've to do is simply use the API to read and write messages.

### 2. Multiple Options

You can either chose the Standard queue or FIFO queue depending upon your requirements.

### 3. Pricing

When you're using Amazon SQS, you only pay for what you use.

### 4. Remove duplication

FIFO queues make sure there aren't any duplicate messages. This makes it suitable for tasks that require each task to be done only once.

## 5. Checks for processing issues

If a message isn't processed, it is sent to the dead-letter queue where you can monitor it.

# Cons of Amazon SQS

## 1. Doesn't support broadcasting

Amazon SQS doesn't allow multiple entities to access the same message, making SQS not so suitable for one to many broadcasts. However, you can use an additional service called SNS along with SQS to enable broadcasting.

## 2. High cost

Although you only have to pay for what you use, if the number of messages you send increases, it will add up to your bill. When thousands of messages are being processed every day, the cost of using the SQS system becomes higher which is an overhead.

# Use cases of Amazon SQS

Amazon SQS can be used in conjunction with other Amazon services such as Amazon EC2, Lambda and Amazon S3. Aside from that, you can use it to send tasks between different components of the system.

Amazon SQS can be used for scheduling batch jobs as it can maintain a queue of all the scheduled jobs so you don't have to track the job status. SQS takes care of handling the system.

Moreover, the service is effective for large distributed workloads where it's important to maintain queues of all tasks needed to be processed and distributed.

## What is the Amazon Simple Workflow Service (SWS)?

Amazon SWF allows you to develop distributed applications by providing a programming model that lets you coordinate work across distributed components. The major concept in Amazon SWF is the workflow. A workflow is a group of activities that have some objective and logic to coordinate the activities. For example, a workflow could be that it receives the customer order and actions will be performed to process the order.

## Terminologies

❖ **Workflow:** A group of activities that have objective along with logic to coordinate the activities.

❖ **Workflow history:** It stores information about the workflow execution/instance. The history includes which activities are being scheduled, their status and results.

❖ **Domain:** Workflow runs in an AWS resource called a domain. An AWS account can have multiple accounts having multiple workflows.

❖ **Activities:** A task to be performed. It's registered with SWF as an activity type along with information such as name, version, and timeout.

❖ **Activity Worker:** It's a program that receives the tasks, performs actions and outputs the results. An activity worker could be either a person or a program.

## How does Amazon SWF work?

When you're designing an Amazon SWF workflow, you've to define the activities and register it with Amazon SWF as an activity type. Specify details such as name, version and timeout values for the activity.

Some activities may need to be carried out more than once. For instance, in a customer order workflow, the customer can buy more than one items and so the activity would run multiple times. This is denoted by an activity task that refers to one invocation of an activity.

An activity worker that receives activity tasks processes it and outputs a result. The task can be performed either by a user using an activity worker software or by the application itself.

The activity tasks are run synchronously or asynchronously. They are distributed amongst multiple networks spread across different regions. They can be written in any high-level programming language and run on any OS.

The logic in a workflow is found in a software program called a decider. The main purpose of the decider is to schedule activity tasks, provides input to the activity workers and process the events.

## What is Amazon Simple Notification Service?

Amazon SNS is a fast and flexible push notification service that allows you to send bulk of messages to a large number of users whether they are mobile device users, subscribers or email recipients. SNS supports multiple end points like http, SQS and email. From the sender's point of view, it's like a single message sent to every type of device and platforms.

Amazon SNS makes use of a publish/subscribe model for the delivery of messages. The subscribers also are known as receivers subscribe to any topic of their interest. The senders (publisher) sends a message to a topic which in turn is delivered to all of the receivers who've subscribed to the topic.

# Terminologies

- ❖ **Topics:** Topics could events, access point, or application that has content. Each topic includes a URL that locates the SNS endpoint.

- ❖ **Subscribers:** Subscribers could be end-users, clients, servers or devices that can receive notifications of any topic.

- ❖ **Owners:** Owners have the authority to create topics and have access control.

- ❖ **Publishers:** Publishers send messages to topics. SNS matches the topic against the subscribers who are found to be interested in the topic and the message is delivered to every subscriber.

## Amazon SNS API

You can use the SNS API to perform various functions:

1. **CreateTopic:** This function lets you create a new topic. The topic name can contain upper and lower case characters, numeric digits and should be up to 256 characters long.

2. **AddPermission:** This function sets up publishers and subscribers having access to the topic.

3. **Subscribe:** The subscribe function includes the information of the subscribers interested in a particular topic.

4. **ConfirmSubscription:** This function allows you to send a confirmation message to the end-user. The subscriber would confirm it by clicking on the link attached in an email.

# Use Cases

## ❖ System Alerts:

System or application alerts are notifications generated when any event occurs such as if there is a change in the system. The notification is sent to the end-users.

## ❖ Push email and SMS:

There are two ways through which message could be transmitted - email and SMS. Amazon SNS is used to target the audience/subscriber through email or text message. The interested audience could then decide to choose whether they want to visit the website or not.

## ❖ Mobile Push Notifications

Amazon SNS is also used for mobile push notifications in which the message is sent to any mobile app by SNS. The notification could be in the form of an update, a newly added feature and other.

# Section 9: Introduction to DNS and AWS Route 53

- ❖ What is Domain Name System?
- ❖ Types of DNS Services
- ❖ What is Amazon Route 53?
- ❖ AWS Route Tables
- ❖ Features of Amazon Route 53
- ❖ Amazon Route 53 APIs
- ❖ How to create a hosted Zone

## What is Domain Name System?

Domain Name System converts domain names into machine-translated IP addresses. It plays a pivotal role when it comes to communication between the end-user and servers. When you're opening a website, you don't have to remember the long IP address, rather you only have to type the URL or the domain name on the tab to access the website.

Amazon offers a DNS service called Amazon Route 53 which is a global service that can translate domain names into IP addresses. The DNS system is similar to the phone directory. The phone book keeps a record of the names with their corresponding phone numbers.

Similarly, the DNS servers have a list of domain names that are mapped into IP addresses, controlling which server the user will access when they type the website name into the browser.

## Types of DNS services

There are two types of DNS services:

1. **Authoritative DNS:**

The authoritative DNS server holds the IP address of the domain name you're searching for. When you're typing a website name into the web browser, a query is sent to the internet service provider (ISP). The ISP has a recursive server that may have the information in its memory. However, if not information is found, the recursive server will have to search for the IP address somewhere else. The authoritative DNS server can get the IP address for the specified domain. Amazon Route 53 is an authoritative DNS.

1. **Recursive DNS:**

Queries aren't directly sent to authoritative DNS service. Instead, they have to go through recursive DNS service which doesn't hold DNS information but can get the IP information on your behalf. If it doesn't find the desired IP address, the query is passed to other authoritative DNS servers.

## What is Amazon Route 53?

Amazon Route 53 is a DNS web service that allows organizations and developers to route the users to their desired application. It converts DNS into IP addresses such as 10.1.0.1.

Amazon Route 53 has powerful policies that allow efficient DNS requests. Once you've your Domain up, you can select the routing policy that meets your needs. The policies are as follows:

### 1. Simple Routing Policy

This is the simplest way of accessing the application server. When you type the website name into the browser, it's translated into IP address.

### 2. Weighted Routing Policy

In this policy, you can assign numeric weights to multiple servers that provide a web service. The traffic is routed to any one server. This type of routing is useful for load balancing.

### 3. Latency based routing policy

In this policy, the traffic is routed to the server having the lowest possible delay. You can run any web-based application across multiple regions and Amazon route 53 will direct users to those servers which are quick and responsive.

### 4. Failover Policy

A failover routing policy sends the traffic to the application server that you set it as primary. As long as the server is healthy, the traffic will be routed, but if it's failing the traffic will be diverted to another server.

### 5. Geo-location Routing

In Geo-location routing, the traffic is directed to the servers based on geographic location. The queries are routed from the specific regions. For example, queries sent from UK are routed to 10.0.0.2 IP address. This means that all of the instances in UK will be routed to this IP address.

## AWS Route Tables

AWS route table consists of a set of rules which are used to find out where the traffic is routed to. All subnets in the VPC are attached to an AWS route table and the table takes control of the routing for those subnets.

## Features of Amazon Route 53

### 1. Traffic flow

You can route traffic to the desired end point on the basis of health, latency, geo-proximity and other metrics.

### 2. Domain Registration

You can easily register for the available domain names using Amazon Route 53. The available domains are .net, .com, .org etc.

### 3. Monitoring Health

AWS Route 53 keeps a check on the health of the applications in case if there are issues in the servers.

### 4. Private DNS

Using Amazon Route 53, you can create private hosted zones that can easily route traffic using manageable domain names within the VPCs. In this way, you can quickly switch between IP based resources without having to update the embedded links.

## Amazon Route 53 APIs

Route 53 has a set of simple APIs that makes it easier to create and manage the DNS records for the domains. You can use these functions using the AWS management console. The commonly used functions are listed below:

1. **CreateHostedZone:** This function allows you to create a new hosted zone to add the DNS data. Once, you've created the hosted zone, you'll receive four name servers to which you can assign to your domain.

2. **DeleteHostedZone:** This function lets you delete a hosted zone.

3. **ChangeResourceRecordSet:** This functions allows you to populate and edit the DNS resources in a particular hosted zone.

4. **CheckAvailability:** This checks the availability of the domain.

## How to Create a Hosted Zone

1. Sign in to the **AWS management console**

2. Go to **services** and click on **Route 53**

3. Go to a domain hosting website that lets you purchase a domain name.

4. Go to the Route 53 dashboard and select **create hosted zone**

5. Specify details such as domain name and set the type as public hosted site.

6. You'll see the values of **name server.** Copy the values and paste it to the custom name servers.

7. Once you've added the name servers, go to change name servers and remove dots at the end of name server values.

8. Create two record sets having type set as "A". The first record set name should be blank while the name for the second record set should be www.

9. Check the domain name by typing it into the browser tab.

www.ingramcontent.com/pod-product-compliance
Lightning Source LLC
LaVergne TN
LVHW041212050326
832903LV00021B/586